ISBN 0-9770500-0-9

A Book By

MICHAEL P. CONNELLY

HOW TO MAKE A MOVIE WITH

A VERY, VERY, LOW BUDGET

- MICHAEL P. CONNELLY -

HOW TO MAKE A MOVIE

WITH A VERY, VERY,

LOW BUDGET

A GUIDE TO MAKING AN INDEPENDENT
FILM ON A SHOESTRING BUDGET

SECOND EDITION

A Uniconn Book – Los Angeles

Copyright 2005   Michael P. Connelly

ISBN 0-9770500-0-9

CONTENTS

• • • • •

| Preface | 14 |

| Introduction | 20 |

1. Writing a Low Budget Script 28

    A great script can level the playing field for you. 28

    You can enjoy creative control. 29

    Tips for writing a low budget script. 30

    Websites that offer script writing services, computer programs and books about writing. 34

2. Buying a Low Budget Script 35

    If you are not a great writer, then hire one. 35

    The best places to buy a low budget script. 35

    Websites that offer info about buying a script. 36

    Tips for buying a low budget script. 36

3. Finding Good, Affordable Actors 39

You can have talented actors in your film. 39

The best way to find good, affordable actors. 40

Websites that offer affordable casting services. 41

How to choose from a large stack of photos and resumes. 41

How much you should pay your actors. 45

4. Location Scouting 48

Choosing locations that save you money. 48

How much you should pay to rent a location. 52

The best types of locations for a low budget film. 53

Tips for conducting a location scouting trip. 54

5. Finding a Good, Affordable Crew 59

How to choose the right kind of crew members. 59

Where to find the best kind of crew members. 64

The right way to negotiate deals with your crew. 66

Web sites that offer information about finding affordable crew members for independent films. 68

Websites that offer information about insurance for film industry equipment. 69

Crew members you need for a bare-bones *run-and-gun* crew and how much to pay them. 78

Recap of the list of 8 suggested crew members. 80

6. Pre-Production 82

The proper amount of pre-production work for a low budget film. 82

How to do a budget breakdown for a low budget film. 83

The best way to do a storyboard for a low budget film. 85

Websites that offer information and software for drawing storyboards. 91

Websites that offer information on finding storyboard artists for hire. 91

How to do a script breakdown for a low budget film. 92

Making a shooting schedule for a low budget film. 94

Pre-production crew meetings, their importance, and how to conduct them. 100

CONTENTS / 10.

Rehearsing with actors, the importance of it, and how it should be done. 103

Release Form/Contracts, their importance, and a sample of how one should look. 104

Information about props and costumes for a low budget film. 108

Important tips for buying film. 112

Link to a web page on Kodak.com for information about buying 16mm film. 116

Crucial information about making travel arrangements for a low budget film shoot. 116

Websites that offer maps and driving directions that will save you time and money. 117

Websites that offer information about the weather that can save you time and money. 119

The right way to plan a low budget film shoot. 121

The best travel related websites for getting good deals on travel arrangements. 124

Tips on buying food and provisions for a low budget film shoot. 125

CONTENTS / 11.

7. Production 130

>The fun part begins, and your film vision starts to become a reality. 130
>
>Production cast and crew meetings, their importance, and how to conduct them. 131
>
>Tips for having a successful low budget film production. 132
>
>Safety tips and information every low budget filmmaker needs to know. 139
>
>Link to AAA website. 143
>
>How to direct a low budget film. 144
>
>Best shooting formula for a low budget film. 152
>
>How to get good performances from actors. 154
>
>Important information about cinematography for low budget films. 155
>
>Important information about doing the sound for a low budget film. 162
>
>How to use props, costumes, and special effects when you are filming a low budget movie. 171

CONTENTS   /   12.

Extremely important information about the storage of film and DAT tapes. 174

8. Post-Production 180

The final phase for making your film vision a reality. 180

Stick to the basics with the post-production phase. 184

Post-production services are much cheaper these days. 185

Websites that offer information about finding post-production services for low budget films. 186

Screening your *dailies*. 187

How to make the *titles* and *credits* for a low budget film. 192

Websites that offer information about people and places that do *titles* and *credits*. 194

The best way to edit a low budget movie. 194

The best way to have your film negative *cut*. 201

Websites that offer information about people and places that *cut* film negatives. 202

Making a *window copy* transfer. 203

Doing sound design/mixing for a low
budget movie without spending too much. 205

Websites with information about people and
places that do post-production sound work. 208

Making 16mm film prints of your movie. 211

Transferring your film to video or DVD. 212

9. Distribution   215

The film festival circuit is the best place
to start. 215

Every movie accepted into one of the prestigious
film festivals has the potential to make it big. 216

Websites that offer information about film
distribution companies. 220

Glossary of Film Industry Terms	222

Index	238

Acknowledgements and References	251

Preface

• • • • •

This book/ebook is available for download on the internet at the website address below.

http://www.makealowbudgetmovie.com/cgi/index.pl?lo=make&s=false

The printed version can also be purchased at this web site by POD (print on demand). While each version has its advantages and disadvantages that could be discussed by a room full of the brightest scholars this world has to offer, the fact remains that the best version is the one that *you* prefer, for whatever reasons *you* choose. Whatever your preferences may be for the version you have chosen, it must be acknowledged that there is one particular obvious limitation that is inherent with the printed version, and that is as follows: any hyperlinks to film industry web sites that are described as being "active" must be accessed by way of a computer and ISP (internet service provider).

A Couple of Notes on the Second Edition

The Second Edition of *How to Make a Movie with a Very, Very Low Budget* contains added information regarding recent and past experiences of mine in the world of independent filmmaking that were not included in the First Edition. I have also added various bits of information regarding events in the film industry and on the film festival circuit, as well as a few more links to film industry related websites that I feel would be very helpful for anyone making a low budget film.

While the general content of the Second Edition is very similar to the First Edition, there are several added anecdotes and bits of information. The main difference is in the format; the original file for the First Edition was designed to be in the AEH format to accommodate easy facilitation of the downloading process of the product file.

There was no special program needed (IE: Adobe Reader) to view or download the file in AEH format. It is a "self-extracting" format and it is for this particular reason that I chose to use it. Basically, anyone with a computer and access to the internet can download it without any problems.

Unfortunately, the AEH format does not accommodate the facilitation of the POD process very easily, and it is for this reason that I chose to design the file of the Second Edition in the PDF format. This particular format requires the use of the *Adobe Reader* program to read the file electronically, but this program can be downloaded for free at www.Adobe.com using any of the links provided on http://www.makealowbudgetmovie.com/cgi/index.pl?lo=make&s=false

It is my belief that it is a mere inconvenience to download this free program, and that the PDF format is the only way to go if you are publishing a book in both electronic and paper form, for it very easily accommodates the facilitation and delivery for both types of product.

Statement of Intent

The purpose of this book is to offer insight into the world of independent filmmaking (on a miniscule budget) through explanations and anecdotes based on my experiences with making low budget films. All of the information in this book is offered in an advisory manner. I am not suggesting in any way that my methods are the *only* ones that can be used to make a movie with a small amount of money, I am only saying that these methods have worked very well for me.

In the past twenty years I have created and produced over fifteen films that ranged from three minute shorts filmed in the Super-8 format, to ninety minute features shot with 16mm film, to several animated shorts that were filmed with 35mm film. With each project I have learned many valuable things that have helped me to get my movies completed with minimum funding. Along with many other things, I have also learned the best ways to get exposure for your film, so that you can ultimately make a profit. I chose the path of the film festival circuit as a springboard to a film career, and it this general idea that I will be stressing throughout this book.

Most of the time the film festival circuit is basically the farm league for the Hollywood film industry (which is a good thing), but sometimes it can also be "the big time". When a movie like *The Blair Witch Project (1999)* comes along and catches the kind of attention that usually is reserved only for the big studio films, this can be considered "the big time". When this happens, the big movie studios stand up and take notice along with the rest of the public. If you have a story that people really enjoy, they will catapult your film from the small towns and venues of the film festival circuit to the worldwide spotlight. Of course, this happens a lot less frequently than it should, but it *does* happen. Most of the films that people go to see at film festivals end up with a decent distribution deal, and an extended life on cable television. You can shoot for the stars, but you must be willing to settle for the upper atmosphere sometimes. This is quite alright though, because the upper atmosphere is a lot better than being on the ground when it comes to the film industry. It is also a shorter distance to the stars from there.

They say that "necessity is the mother of invention", and I have had a career that exemplifies this statement in every way. I have always been the kind of person who has had an abundance of creative ideas with only a minimum amount of funding to make them happen, but that never stopped me. I tend to do my best work under pressure, and there is no pressure in the world like trying to finish a movie with a miniscule budget. You have an idea that you have sold to a bunch of people and you have to make a film production happen or you will not only lose the money you are investing, but you will also lose respect from all the people involved with your film project. There have been some good ideas born in the heat of the low budget film production battle, and some bad ones too. The good part about it is now I know what to include and exclude when it comes to my methods. All of the material in the following pages is the stuff that I considered to be the most relevant and helpful when it comes to making a low budget film.

PREFACE /   18.

The bottom line with this book is that it can show you that it is possible to make *your* film dream a reality, and defy the general impression that it takes millions of dollars to make a good movie. If you follow my instructions, and use my methods, you too can complete a film with a lot less money than you think. I am not going to assume that it will be a *good* movie, for that part is entirely up to you and your creative ideas, as well as how efficient you are at executing your plan.

I approached this project with more of a technical and logistical point of view than I did from a creative one. My intent with this book is to give the reader information that can be helpful for making a low budget movie, *not* to give ideas for *good* movies. The creative part is up to you.

It is my hope that all who read this book will take away a certain amount of knowledge that they just could not find anywhere else in any other book. The information contained in this book is not taught in any film class anywhere in the world. It comes straight from my own experiences as a low budget filmmaker. Sometimes, my methods may seem to contradict things that are taught in film schools or film production books. My only defense in these cases is that my methods are products of many years of trial and error, and they work for me.

I have spent many years learning many different things about making movies, and I learned most of my lessons from the school of hard knocks. There have been moments of complete failure and disappointment mixed in with moments of shear jubilation and success, and I have accepted them all with the idea in mind that every moment was a learning experience of some kind. This book is the product of those experiences, and it can serve as a guide to navigating the rough waters of a low budget film production.

While the general formula for making a movie is a relatively simple process, the business side of the film industry these days has made it seem very complex. Most people who dream of making a movie get scared away from the idea by the misconception that it costs way more money than they could possibly raise for a film project. With this book, I am telling you that it does not need to be a complex process. If you have an abundance of creativity, a small budget, a burning desire to make your ideas happen, and a dash of ingenuity, then you can make any movie idea come to fruition. This book will help you avoid the many pitfalls that can sink a low budget film production. After you read it, you will be armed with the knowledge you need to make your movie a reality. The rest is up to you.

Introduction

· · · · ·

    Congratulations! You are one step closer to fulfilling your dream.

    If you are reading this book it means that you have a dream to make a movie. In the very least, you have been wondering what it would be like to dabble in the business of independent filmmaking. Well, you have just bought a book that will give you all the information you need to make that dream a reality.

    There is good news in the world of filmmaking; for anyone who has ever had a dream to make a movie, now is the time to act. There is a growing trend in the film industry that favors anyone who wants to make their own low budget film. Recently there has been a shift in popularity from big-budget commercialized films, to low-budget personalized films. Film audiences are fed up with the formulaic films that the major studios have been spoon-feeding them for years, and they are hungry for good stories.

    There is a myth that has persisted for years that says a person needs millions of dollars to make a movie. This is quite simply not true. While it is true that most of the movies you see in the theaters today cost on the average about 50 million dollars to make, it is not the cost of actually *making* the movie that is so expensive. Most of the money for these movies goes to "above the line" salaries (Big name Stars, Directors, writers, etc...), and not to the actual physical production of the movie. For instance, Tom Cruise and Jim Carrey demand 20 million dollars to star in a movie, and they are only one piece of the puzzle. Add an expensive director, writer, etc... and you can see why some of these movies can cost up to 150 million dollars. It really doesn't cost this much to make a film.

The fact of the matter is, if you take away the expensive price tags, the big film studios are just using the same general process that the guy who makes a movie for $50,000 uses to produce his film. Both use camera equipment and sound equipment to capture actors telling a story. The big studio films just have a lot more bells and whistles. If you cut away the fat on a film production, you can make a movie for a lot less than you think.

The general public has been taught to believe that movies cost millions of dollars to make. Yes, some do cost over 150 million dollars to make, but those movies are not the ones that distributors are hoping to purchase when they attend the many film festivals that are out there these days. They are looking for films like *Clerks* by Kevin Smith, or *The Blair Witch Project.* Both of these movies were made for practically nothing, both were hits at the *Sundance Film Festival,* and both films were springboards to major careers in the film industry for the makers of the films.

It is true that not all small films end up making it to the big time through the film festival circuit. Only the standouts from the crowd get major attention. However, there are still a lot of movie deals made that you never hear about that give the makers of small films a decent profit, and a chance to do other projects. The appetites of the cable and satellite television channels are voracious, and they are always looking for material to fill their programming schedules. Distributors feed the hungry entertainment industry with previously undiscovered films that come out of the film festival circuit.

Of course, you must have a decent product to get attention. There are many variables involved in the success of a low budget movie (or any movie), and I will not pretend that I know the magic formula to making a successful film. What I do know is that passion is the most important variable in the success of any film project, and if you can bring that to the table, along with a general knowledge of film production, and a little money, you stand a good chance of success.

The bottom line is: A movie is just a story on film, and it doesn't have to cost millions of dollars to get a story put on film. Yes, there are certain expensive costs that cannot be avoided like film stock and lab processing, but the majority of the work done on a film is labor. This part can be negotiated down and bargained for to save you a lot of money.

There have been some amazing success stories coming out of the film festival circuit in the last two decades. Some filmmakers have had their careers sky rocket to success after entering extremely low-budget films in film festivals. The trend started in the early nineties with films like *Laws of Gravity* by Nick Gomez. This film was shot with a budget of only $38,000, but it won several awards at major festivals and led to jobs for this young, talented filmmaker on real movies, with real (expensive) budgets. *The Living End* is a movie that cost only $22,769 to make, but ended up making a career for Gregg Araki after his film garnered several awards at major film festivals.

El Mariachi is an extreme example of a movie that was made on a shoestring budget and then went on to achieve considerable box office success. The budget for this film was only $7,225, but it ended up getting a lot of attention at the Sundance Film Festival. It later went on to achieve box-office success in theaters nationwide after it was purchased by a major studio, then blown up to a 35mm print. In this case, Robert Rodriguez boasted that he made his film with only a two-man crew, and used friends with no acting experience as his actors. Soon after the success of this film he went on to write and direct several big studio films that included *From Dusk Til' Dawn*, *Spy Kids*, and *Sin City*. In all of the above mentioned cases, the filmmakers were at a great disadvantage due to budget constraints, but they were able to do whatever it took to get their movies made, and it paid off for them.

The only thing a person needs to get a movie made is an undying determination to fulfill their dream. If you have a burning desire to make movies, as I have had since I was a child, then you will get the job done, no matter what it takes (as long as it is legal and ethically sound).

Everybody has a story that they have always wanted to tell, and making a movie is a good way to tell it. The word *magic* has always been associated with the film industry, and while some people consider the technical achievements of filmmakers to be the magic part of films, I am of the belief that the *story* part of a movie is the *real* magic. *ET: The Extraterrestrial* did not capture our hearts with his technologically advanced gadgets; it was the story that drew us in. While that movie did have a pretty big budget, my point is that it did not need to have one in order to succeed. You should not be afraid to have great expectations for your film if you *really* believe in the story. Who knows, maybe your story is a lot more interesting than you think, and if people at a film festival agree with this notion, then your story could take off.

As I stated in the Preface, the purpose of this book is to give you tips and information that will show you how to make a movie with a very, very, low budget (by Hollywood's standards). The kind of budget that I am talking about should be around $50,000. A film can be made for less than that amount, but using experience as my yardstick I have found that it takes at least that much money to make a movie that has a professional-looking production value, is shot on film, and can be presented to film festivals on a 16mm film print. There are certain production value standards that are required even of the small films in order to be purchased by a distributor and it will cost you about that much to live up to those standards.

There is always the option to shoot on video (which can be done for practically nothing), but this book is all about shooting on film, and doing it inexpensively. Ninety-nine percent of the movies you see in the theaters, at film festivals, and on television are shot on film. The digital revolution has yet to make film obsolete because film still has the best image quality available. If you want to be in the game, you need to play by the rules, and right now the rules still say you need to shoot on film.

I will not be giving any advice on how to secure your budget, for I am not an expert on financial matters. I must assume that you are capable of securing the budget on your own. Below are two links that give information on how to get funding for a film.

- http://www.fundingfilm.com/

- http://www.northernvisions.org/funding.htm

I am also assuming that you have a general knowledge of the process of film production. Whether you learned it in film school or you are self taught, a basic knowledge of filmmaking is required to take advantage of the information in this book. Even the most passionate storyteller must have skills to relate their story to others and in this case those skills require that you know the basics of film production.

For those of you who are not yet educated on the process of filmmaking I have provided three links below to websites that offer information on learning the fundamentals of film production.

- http://www.webfilmschool.com/

- http://www.nyfa.com/

PREFACE   /   26.

- http://www.lafilm.com/

The keys to getting a movie made with a small amount of money are promotion, multi-tasking and making deals for services. You must be an avid promoter of your movie before, during, and after the film production process. You must tirelessly sell people on the beneficial aspects for them if they are involved in the making of your film such as exposure, and a chance to have a product in "The Game" that has their name in the main credits.

You can get a lot of really good professional film industry people to work for pennies and even double-up on jobs if you offer them creative control during the production process. Most importantly, you must make them believe that your movie will benefit their careers. In order for this to work, everyone must agree that this film has potential, and could be a stepping stone to bigger and better things. They must also agree to do more than one job, and work for very little money. In some cases, deferred payment deals can be made if the person really believes in your film.

The key to finding talented people to work cheaply is knowing where to look. In my many years of frequenting equipment rental houses, film labs, post-production houses, film industry websites, and any other places that have to do with the making of a film, I have learned where to find these people. I will tell you all about it in the pages to follow.

For anyone who has studied the process of filmmaking and dreamed of making a movie, this book is for you.

PREFACE   /   27.

In this book you will find valuable information about the best ways to get your movie made on a shoestring budget.

   Once your story is put to film, anything is possible. It could take on a life of it's own and open the door to a career in the film industry, it could bring you a profit from a distribution deal, or it could lead to the fulfillment of a dream to make a movie and enter it in a film festival. Whatever happens, I do know that this book will help you better understand that a movie can be made for a lot less money than you ever thought possible.

   Thank you for your interest in my book and I hope you have as much fun reading it as I had writing it.

   Keep your dreams alive and never let your creative vision fade.

Michael P. Connelly

www.makealowbudgetmovie.com/cgi/index.pl?lo=make&s=false

Copyright 2005. Michael P. Connelly

1

Writing a Low Budget Script

This step is by far the most important factor in making a successful low-budget movie. This is where you can make up for your lack of slick production value by making the audience focus on an involving story. The playing field is level for everyone when it comes to writing a good story. No-one has a monopoly on creativity. All you have to do is put your idea down on paper (in script format), officially register it, and then begin showing it to people who work in the film industry. If your script is good, people will be drawn to it. Once people start to back your idea, there's a good chance your movie will get made.

Writing for me has always been the most enjoyable part of the filmmaking process. This is where thoughts become reality, and your film idea is no longer just "talk". I consider myself much more of a creative type than a technical person, so this is where the real me comes out.

I wrote, directed, and produced every film that I have ever made. These three positions alone are usually three different people on a major studio film, and it would cost millions of dollars to pay for the salaries. If you have the ability to do these three jobs yourself, you are halfway to having your movie made on a small budget.

WRITING A LOW BUDGET SCRIPT   /   29.

While taking on these three responsibilities can be a daunting task, it can also give you complete creative control. That is the up side of doing a low budget movie. You have the freedom to bring your vision to reality without the usual financial backers telling you how they want to change your script to fit their idea of what a "successful movie" should have in the storyline.

Enjoy the creative control when you write your low budget script, because you might not have it later on when other people are financing your movie with big dollars. The more money involved, the more control you will lose in the creative process. But don't be discouraged. If your career takes off, you will gradually get creative control back.

As much as the major studios have tried to find a script formula that works every time to make a hit movie, they continue to fail. The collective consciousness of the movie going public is as unpredictable as earthquake forecasting. What was popular with audiences yesterday may not be popular today. There have been many times in the history of filmmaking that studios have invested millions of dollars in a movie project that they thought would be a hit, only to find that the movie failed miserably at the box office. While this unpredictability has been known to cause movie studio executives to lose their jobs, it has also been responsible for launching the careers of many previously unknown filmmakers.

A good, original script is a low-budget filmmaker's most valuable asset. The script is the anchor of the creative process in a film production. If you can write a really good script, your movie project will take on a life of it's own.

WRITING A LOW BUDGET SCRIPT / 30.

Creative types (and people in general) just love a good story. As the saying goes, "everyone has a story", and if you can put your awesome story onto paper (in script format, of course) for people to read, you can rally them around your cause. If you move them, they will be moved to jump on board with you to get your movie made. Once the story is made into a film, then you have the opportunity to move people at film festivals, which will move them to create a *buzz* about your film, which of course, is never a bad thing.

If you are writing the script yourself, make sure you are totally satisfied with it before you proceed any further with your film project. Make sure the storyline is tight, and it is as good as you can possibly make it.

Submit your script to other creative types to read, and then ask them for feedback. Be open-minded to criticism and suggested changes, but stay loyal to your original story idea. Be sure to register your idea with the WGA first.

Tips for Writing a Low Budget Script:

• 1. Write a character-driven story that is mainly about one or two people.

• 2. Write about a topic that interests you greatly, and write from the heart. Lay your feelings on the page with every ounce of skill and emotion you possess. Draw on your real life experiences for material. Life truly is stranger than fiction sometimes. Remember, this is your best chance to connect with your audience. It is all about STORYLINE.

WRITING A LOW BUDGET SCRIPT   /   31.

Visuals are important, but storyline is king in independent films.

• 3. Write about topics that push people's emotional buttons (IE: a person's life struggle against all odds, a story of undying love, a controversial political topic, etc...).

• 4. Do not include a lot of explosions or special effects, as these take a lot of time, effort, and money.

• 5. Do not write a story that requires a lot of period costumes, as these can also cost you a lot of time, effort, and money.

• 6. Do not write scenes that require a lot of extras, or children (expensive and difficult).

• 7. Keep your cast small in numbers. 5-7 people maximum as your primary actors.

• 8. Write more EXTERIOR scenes than INTERIOR scenes into your script to avoid costly and time-consuming lighting set-ups. Reflectors are a lot quicker and easier to use than lights are, and they do not require electricity to operate.

• 9. Write scenes that can be shot using mostly *available light* (the sun).

• 10. Write scenes that involve desolate wilderness. Desert and mountain areas can offer stunning settings that can be written into your story. Wilderness locations have a much more relaxed atmosphere than urban or suburban locations. Away from the public, wilderness locations allow everyone to be creative without pressure or distractions. Also, film permits are obsolete in some areas where no-one is around but you and your small outfit.

• 11. Do your location scouting before you write the final draft of your script so you can write scenes that have locations close to each other. This will save you a lot of time and money by allowing you to shoot and then move on to the next location quickly. Choose locations that are on public land, as you would much rather deal with a nosy park ranger than you would an angry property owner that happens to come along. When they see how small your outfit is, they sometimes don't press the issue of film permits.

• 12. Do not write too many complicated camera moves into your scenes, as these take a lot of time to rehearse and execute properly. Remember, time is money.

• 13. Keep your script fairly short. 80-90 pages max. This will save you time and money because it means fewer pages for the script supervisor to deal with which means less work for them to do. You can pack a lot of story into a short script if you eliminate a lot of the technical details that go with a big budget action movie.

• 14. And most importantly, be ORIGIONAL. Don't take the easy way out by writing just another rehash of something that has already been done before. Remember, your script is the roadmap for your film vision, and if you want that vision to get attention from others, it must be unique.

• 15. Research your topic thoroughly. Don't assume that people won't know the difference between historical accuracy and a wild guess about the date of something, a certain style of clothing, the name of a town, etc... If you are wrong, you can create a negative *buzz* about your film when people expose your inaccuracies. Don't jeopardize the success of your film with a lack of research.

• 16. Make sure you are passionate about the topic you choose to write about. You are going to be living, eating, and breathing this project for at least a year of your life, so think long and hard about what you want to write about before you start, then; jump into it with a passion.

• 17. Do not write too many scenes with different locations. Make the most of every location. Chooses places that have several different looks available for a variety of scenes. For example, you could choose a house or building that is on the edge of a wilderness area so you could shoot exterior wilderness scenes in the day time and interior scenes at night without having to pack up and repo everyone to another location.

• 18. If you feel that you are not a strong enough script writer to do your story justice, then hire a script writer to write your script. You can find one at the links below. Ask for samples of their writing, and then choose the one that shows strong character driven writing skills.

Websites that offer script writers for hire:

- http://www.guru.com/
- http://www.writesight.com/

Websites that offer computer programs for writing screenplays:

- http://www.finaldraft.com/
- http://www.scriptware.com/

Websites that offer books, CDs, and courses on script writing:

- http://www.writequickly.com/?afl=13672
- http://www.writers-block-cd.com/?afl=13672
- http://www.writingclasses.com/index.php

2

Buying a Low Budget Script

If you do not have a strong talent for screenplay writing, then your best bet is to buy a script from a talented writer that has yet to get their "big break". You may have a good story to tell, but if you cannot tell it in script format and with a visual style, then you will have a hard time convincing people it is a good story for a film.

A good script can be obtained for only a few thousand dollars from a hungry, talented writer that just wants to see their work committed to film.

Here are a couple of good ways to buy a low budget script:

- 1. Place a "scripts wanted" classified ad on one of the many film industry related websites that are on the internet. You will get a lot of replies, and many scripts to choose from.

- 2. Look on the many websites that are out there that offer "Scripts For Sale" on "spec"(freelance).

Websites that will be helpful to anyone searching for a script to buy:

BUYING A LOW BUDGET SCRIPT   /   36.

- http://www.simplyscripts.com/links.html

- http://www.filmmakers.com/member/screenwriter/

- http://www.mandy.com/

Tips for buying a script for a low budget film:

• 1. Look for scripts that have the same qualities as the ones I mentioned in the section about writing a low budget script (IE: character-driven story, small cast, simple costumes, outdoor locations, etc...) on page 4.

• 2. Use the 5 PAGE METHOD when reading through the scripts: if the story has not been firmly established and you are not completely hungry to learn more after reading 5 pages, then toss the script and move on to the next one.

• 3. Remember, STORYLINE is paramount in choosing your script. It must be interesting, moving, and tightly written.

• 4. Take your time and read all that are worth reading (don't rush through them). If it passes the "5 page" test, then it's usually worth reading to the end. You don't want to miss an undiscovered gem of a script just because a few pages in the middle are weak. Read all the way to the end the ones that start out strong.

• 5. Tell the writers who send you scripts to include a brief bio/resume.

- 6. Choose the best script that was written by an unknown writer with talent (there are a lot of them out there). This type of writer will be much more willing to make compromises to fit your budget than an established writer would.

- 7. Ask the script writer how much money they want for their script. Do not make the first offer. This is an old sales tactic that could save you a lot of money. Chances are the writer is going to start with a very low price if they have not sold any scripts yet.

- 8. If the writer wants more than five thousand dollars, then tell them about the many other scripts you have to consider, and that all of them are selling for much less.

- 9. Tell the script writer your plans to enter your film in festivals like *Sundance,* and that it would be great exposure for them that could lead to bigger and better deals if the film does well.

- 10. Explain to the writer that everyone who plans to work on your film has agreed to do so with the understanding that this film can be a valuable stepping-stone to a better career and that no-one is asking for what they are really worth.

- 11. If you have any awards for short films, show them to the script writer. This will show you have experience with film festivals (your first target audience), and that you have done well.

- 12. Offer the script writer a very prominent credit in your film (and on the poster) in exchange for lowering his price.

- 13. If you do not feel that it is necessary to make many changes in the script you choose, then tell the script writer that his story will not be altered in any way. Creative control is a luxury that every writer wants in their career.

- 14. Take your time to decide on which script you want to buy. Once again, the script is your strongest asset in a low budget film, so make sure you choose something you feel is totally original, and gripping. Remember, this film project is going to be your life for at least a year, so choose a script wisely. The last thing you want to do is spend good money on a script that you thought looked good on the surface, but turned out to be not what you thought it was once you took a closer look. If you make a bad decision with a script purchase, you either have to make a movie you do not really feel like making, or throw the script away and buy another one. Neither choice sounds good, so be sure that you read a script thoroughly before you buy it.

3

Finding Good, Affordable Actors

Just because you are making a low budget movie it doesn't mean you can't have good, quality actors in your film. There are plenty of hungry actors out there who are ready to sink their teeth into your script just to get a chance to practice their craft (and get paid a little). All you have to do is advertise in the right place, and you will get a flood of actors sending you their "head-shot" photos and resumes. Acting really is one of the most competitive lines of work there is, and this can work to your advantage. One small ad placed in the right publication will bring all kinds of actors, both good, and bad, running to your project in earnest (especially if there is pay involved). The hard part will be choosing which ones would be best for your film.

If you advertise in a major city like New York or Los Angeles, you might get thousands of replies, so be ready to make a trip to your post office every day to pick up your boxes full of large envelopes from actors. One time I advertised that I was looking for actors in the main actors trade magazine in Hollywood (CA), and I not only received over a dozen boxes at my local post office full of photos and resumes, but they kept rolling in for months until they finally faded away about six months later. The postal employees at my local post office were sick of me by the

FINDING GOOD, AFFORDABLE ACTORS   /   40.

time it was over, and it took me weeks to sort through all the replies I received.

Here is the best way to find good, affordable actors:

Advertise in the main actor's trade magazine of the largest city close to where you live.

1. Go to the largest newspaper/magazine stand in town and ask for actor's trade magazines/newspapers.

2. Choose the one that seems to be the biggest publication (IE; *Backstage West* in CA), buy it, and bring it home.

3. Go to the back of the newspaper/magazine and read through the classified ads to see what kind of ads they offer.

4. Contact the newspaper and place an "actors wanted" ad that describes your project (low budget film) and the parts you are looking to cast. At the end of the ad state: SOME PAY and VHS/DVD.

5. Go to your post office EVERY DAY to pick up your mail until the replies taper off.

   You can also find a lot of hungry, talented actors on the internet at various different websites that cater to people who are looking to cast their films. You can place a classified ad on the websites, you can search through photos and resumes of actors that are posted on the sites, or you can hire people to do the casting process for you at a reasonable price.

FINDING GOOD, AFFORDABLE ACTORS   /   41.

Websites that offer casting services for television and film projects:

http://www.thedailycall.com/

http://www.abcasting.net

   The next thing you have to do is choose the right actors for your movie. This is very, very important. Not only do these actors have to be able to act, but they also have to be able to do their own make-up (if they want it), along with a variety of other chores that actors are not traditionally expected to do. Most importantly, they must be easy to work with, and they must be reliable. The last thing you want to do is hire an actor that gives you nothing but trouble on the set, even worse, doesn't even show up on the set at all on some days!

   The most talented or most experienced actor is not necessarily the best actor for your movie if they are hard to work with, or unwilling to compromise. You are going to be working long days in multiple locations sometimes, and they have to be capable of keeping up with you and your fast-moving crew without complaining.

Follow the steps below to find the best actors for your movie:

1. Sort through your piles of photos first and make a short stack for each movie part you are casting based on the *look* you had in mind (does their appearance match your vision). You could spend months interviewing every single person (no matter what they look like) to eliminate all doubts in

FINDING GOOD, AFFORDABLE ACTORS   /   42.

your mind that you found the best actors for your movie, but time is money, and chances are you will find a suitable actor in each of your short stacks of photos that are based on the *look* you had in mind. As shallow as it sounds, the *look* is the best place to start when you are deciding on criteria for your short stacks of actor's photos.

2. Save all the photos and resumes you receive until you have cast the movie.

3. Go through each stack one at a time and read each resume that is attached (or on the back of) each photo.

You are looking for actors that have:

1. An impressive amount of professional training (a degree in acting from a noted university or performing arts school, extensive training from acting classes or workshops, etc...), for these are the ones that are the most serious about acting, and best suited for a character-driven storyline.

2. As much experience on other film projects as possible. More than likely, they know the routine about working on low budget films if they have any experience at all. This will make the negotiation process less of a task.

3. Any actor with any kind of name recognition. Sometimes you will get actors you have actually heard of sending you a photo and resume. This could be due to a variety of reasons that range from; the actor just loved your story idea, to they just haven't worked in a while. You don't care about why they want to be in your movie, you just want to take advantage of their name recognition to attract people to see it. Of course, they have to be right for the part before

FINDING GOOD, AFFORDABLE ACTORS / 43.

you try to sign them up. Your advertisement made it clear that you are working with a low budget, so if an actor you've heard of sends their photo and resume, they obviously understand that there is not a lot of pay involved with the deal.

4. Once you have nailed down your short stacks of actors photos and resumes for each part you are casting, its time to take it a step further. Contact each actor by email and ask them to send you a VHS or DVD copy of their acting "reel". Look for actors with reels that show strong performances in roles that resemble the part they are up for in your movie. Even if the samples they provide were only small parts, look for STRONG PERFORMANCES.

5. After you have viewed all the "reels" narrow your choices down to about five people for each part. Make a first choice, second choice, third choice, etc... for each part.

6. Contact each of your final five choices by phone and do a phone interview in which you discuss:

- A. Your standard payment deal (VHS/DVD copy of the film and daily pay) according to your low budget pay scale.

- B. Their availability to shoot during your projected shooting schedule time.

- C. How they feel about working on a low budget film:

    - a. Are they disdainful, or respectful of projects like yours?

b. Are they enthusiastic about the chance to have some creative control, or are they just looking to add more volume to their acting "reel" (obviously, you are looking for enthusiastic people).

c. Are they willing to work for less pay than they are worth?

D. Availability and willingness to rehearse extensively for at least 2 weeks before filming begins.

E. A willingness to work long, hard hours, and move quickly from one location to the next during the shooting process.

7. Next, you must meet with your final choices in person and have an impromptu "cold reading" of a sample from your script. Meet with each actor separately at a different time and location so that you can show that your undivided attention is on them. A park is a good neutral location to meet. Again, look for STRONG PERFORMANCES even in "cold readings".

8. Finally, choose your cast, and start planning to rehearse the entire script.

Like any other artist, an actor needs to practice their craft in order to improve their skills. Serious actors usually try to keep working in any way they can to stay in touch with their art form (while they are struggling to make a name for themselves), which means they try to work on as many projects as possible. They understand that the money is not there on the small, independent films, and they are willing

FINDING GOOD, AFFORDABLE ACTORS   /   45.

to make that concession in return for a chance to work as an actor on a film, as long as you provide them with a VHS or DVD copy of the film to prove it. Actors are always trying to build their acting "reels" and your movie may be a chance to do just that with the VHS/DVD copy you provide them with.

   The agreement to give a copy of the final version of your film on VHS or DVD is your greatest bargaining tool you have to get good actors to work on your film. This is in fact your greatest bargaining tool with most of the people that you will work with on a low budget movie. In essence you are saying I will put up the money, time, and effort to make a movie and you can showcase your talents if you will agree to forget about most of the money part of the equation, and all of the luxuries.

This brings us to the money issue:

How much do you pay your actors?

   The general idea is that you are not paying them what they are worth, but just what they will accept as a bottom line. Experience, talent, and popularity of the actor does not come into play here like with bigger movies and everyone involved must understand this in order for an agreement to be made.

Here is the standard deal that you should offer all actors in your low budget movie:

1. Film credit (and title for principal actors).

FINDING GOOD, AFFORDABLE ACTORS   /   46.

2. A VHS or DVD copy of your film upon completion of the final product.

3. Daily pay:

   A. Principal cast members- $75/day

   B. Supporting cast members- $40/day

   C. Extra cast members (extras) - $10/day

Some actors may take offense at this pay scale, and if they do, then remind them of the stack of other actor's resumes you still need to go through, and that you must be going now. It sounds cold, but that is the reality of the situation. The number of Screen Actors Guild members who are actually employed on a regular basis is something like 10%. The film industry is a cold place to work unless you are on top, and everyone struggling to get there understands that it is feast or famine, so I wouldn't worry too much about hurting people's feelings with your low-ball pay scale. The reality is; working in your small movie is better than no movie.

If necessary, explain to actors that the main idea here is them getting a chance to be in a movie, and all they have to do is show up on the set locations and do their job, while you and your crew will do the rest of the work. Tell them that you will provide food and hotel rooms when necessary, as well as any other basic needs associated with doing their job as an actor in your movie.

FINDING GOOD, AFFORDABLE ACTORS

Most people who work in the film industry, especially struggling actors, understand your budget constraints. They understand that the most important thing is just getting the movie made so everyone involved can add another credit to their film "reels" and show off their skills. If they don't understand the big picture, then simply move on to the next candidate. Don't waste your time with people that ask for more money than you can pay, because the reality of the situation is you can't afford to negotiate. You have to work with a very lean, fixed pay scale, or you will run out of money before you get your first" work-print" finished.

4

Location Scouting

This is another very important part of your pre-production process. Extensive location scouting is a vital part of saving you money on a low budget movie because it can save you a lot of time if you choose the right locations. The "right" locations in this case are any ones that not only have the look you had in mind, but are also in close proximity to each other.

Choosing locations close to each other saves you money for the following reasons:

1. You will be able to move your cast and crew from one location to another very quickly, which eliminates costly time you would have to spend packing, unpacking and in transit (once again, time is money!).

2. You will be able to shoot more scenes in a single day which will shorten the number of total days in your shooting schedule, which means less money you have to pay for everyone and their expenses.

No matter how much you enjoy working with your cast and crew, the bottom line is; the less time spent with them on this film, the better, because every minute spent with them costs you money. You want to get this film "in the can" as quickly as possible, without compromising your vision or the production value too much. Thorough location scouting will help you achieve this goal, and it will save you money.

When you are searching for locations it is always best to start in places that are not too far away from where you and the majority of the people working on your film live. The idea here is to avoid costly hotel and travel expenses for cast and crew.

Location scouting is also a very important part of the creative process. You are basically supplying the canvas for your artists to work on when you choose the location of a scene. It will ultimately define the look of your film in a major way, so you should always choose interesting locations.

A brilliant wilderness location can become a character in the movie when used in a man vs. nature story. In the classic movie *Deliverance (1972),* the river and the rugged wilderness were not only the setting, but they where also part of the story. A power company was planning to build a dam that would flood the entire wilderness area, thus destroying it, so the nature location itself played the biggest victim in this movie. It also allowed for some very impressive cinematography that showed the fury and unforgiving nature of the wilderness. Of course there were the hillbillies, but nature ended up being the real villain in that movie, and it all started with a good location scout to find the ideal place to shoot.

LOCATION SCOUTING   /   50.

Location scouting can be very fun and exiting. It gives you a chance to travel around and see all sorts of different places that you probably would not have seen if you were not making a movie. I have been in some very unique places on some of my location scouts. One time I backpacked up Mount Ranier in Washington to find a location that included a snow-capped volcano. Another time I camped in the middle of the desolate Baja California desert to find a location that included the rare "cholla cactus" (the big ones that you used to see in old cartoons).

If you are looking for city locations to shoot at, the best thing to do is to choose an area that has a good (and safe) place to park your car in a PAID PARKING STRUCTURE. Feeding a parking meter is not a good idea, for you do not know how long you will be searching, and the last thing you want is an expensive parking ticket cutting into your budget. It is much better to pay the $5 to the parking attendant and have all day to walk around without worrying about getting back to your car to feed the parking meter. Also, your car and equipment are a lot safer in a paid parking structure/lot than they are parked on a city street. I had my car broken into before on a street in Los Angeles when I was on a location scout, so I learned the hard way. I lost a video camera, CDs, clothing, and it cost me $200 to fix the broken window. That was an expensive mistake.

Choose locations wisely

If you see a particular store or building that would be good for one of the INTERIOR scenes of your movie, then walk inside and look around, all the while feeling out the

LOCATION SCOUTING / 51.

situation. First, say "hello" and see how they react. If they give you a mug-faced reply or no reply at all, then chances are they are not very nice people. Also, see how they treat their customers and people around them as you are strolling around. You are looking for nice people to deal with, not angry, miserable people. It is amazing how much you can tell about a person just by saying "hello" to them. Look for jovial, friendly people, and you will have a much better chance of working out a deal to film at their location. Also, a quick character assessment of a person is crucial before you put your head on the chopping block with your proposal. Is this person treating their customers and co-workers fairly? Does this person seem reliable on the surface? The last thing you want is to plan a shoot, get your cast and crew to show up, only to find out that the creep you made a deal with has changed his mind about letting you film there. You will lose a lot of money if this happens, for you still have to pay your cast and crew for that day, even if you don't shoot. Try to choose people to deal with who seem like good people.

When you decide to approach a person in a location that you want to film at you should always do it at the beginning of the day. People are usually in a better mood in the morning than they are at the end of a day because they are fresh and untainted by the problems that come with a day of working and living in the city. Always wait until they are not busy with a customer, or anything else.

The first thing you want to do when asking someone about filming at their place is talk to the owner (or the manager if owner is not present) and tell them about your film project. Make sure you emphasize to them that you are

LOCATION SCOUTING   /   52.

working with a VERY, VERY, SMALL BUDGET, so they don't think you are representing some big Hollywood Studio. Then ask them if they would be willing to let you film in their location on DAYS THAT THEY ARE CLOSED, or BEFORE/AFTER HOURS of regular business. Tell them that you will not disturb or alter their location in any way, and that you have a very small cast and crew.

This is the standard payment deal you should offer anyone to use their location for shooting your film:

1. $100/day.

2. An agreement (in writing) to give them a "special thanks to..." film credit at the end of the movie in which you mention their name and location.

　　As for EXTERIOR city locations, my advice is to choose the ones where you won't be right in the middle of public. Try to choose a street that is not too populated, but has a good view of the city behind it as a background. In film school I was taught that you should never shoot on a public street without first securing a film permit through the local film commission office. My professors claimed that if you get caught filming without a permit, it will cost you a lot more in fines and money lost from a cancelled film shoot, than it would to pay the fee for the permit in the first place. Well, I have found that this is just not true.

　　If you get in quickly, film, and get out quickly, the chances of getting caught by a film commission person (who actually cares about you and your small outfit) is very slim. In fact, in all the places I have ever shot in public, I have never been accosted by anyone who asked me for a film permit. As long as you keep your cast and crew *very* small and fast on their feet, and you stay low-key, you can shoot at just about any public street without a permit. These permits are designed to make money off of movies that have a "real" budget, not from very small, independent films. In any case, shooting on a public street should be your last choice for locations, unless you absolutely need it.

Private property and wilderness are best choices

Whether you are looking for a stunning view or a man-made structure, it is always best to shoot on private property that is owned by someone you know (or just met). This will save you the hassle and money it takes to get a film permit and it will give you much more flexible rules to play by, such as amount of time you are allowed to spend shooting on a particular location, how many days, etc... Dealing with people you know is a lot easier than dealing with some film commission official whose primary goals are to bring money and recognition to their town by selling film permits.

Most people that you approach regarding the use of their property for filming a movie are very receptive to the idea. Some are even exited about it. Deep down inside I believe that almost everyone has a dream or desire to be part of the making of a movie, no matter how small the movie. It seems interesting and fun to them. Besides, you will not be disrupting their business in any way, and they can make a little extra cash at the same time.

Bring Cameras

Take a still camera with you on your location scouting trip and take plenty of photos of the locations you visit. Even if you are not quite sure you will use a certain location, it is a good idea to take a photo of it. If something interests you in any way at all, take a picture of it. You will have plenty of time later when you are poring over your photos to decide whether or not you like that location enough to put it in your. It is a lot cheaper to pull a photo out of your computer or file cabinet than it is to revisit a location, so do not hesitate to take a lot of pictures when you are on a location scout.

It is also a good idea to bring a video camcorder with you on any location scouting trips. While still photos give you a good idea of what a shot will look like, you can actually practice the camera moves for some shots with a camcorder.

Bring a data recorder

You should also bring something for writing notes about each location. If you don't have an electronic device like a laptop/notebook computer or a PDA, then bring a small paper notebook or notepad. Write notes that include such things as the directions to the location, number of foreseeable problems associated with the location (IE; difficult access, unknown owner of property, etc...), and anything else that might help you decide later if the location is good for filming.

Stay true to your vision

LOCATION SCOUTING   /   55.

   Having locations that are nearby is an important factor, but it is more important to not compromise your film vision just to have a location that is close to where everyone working on the movie lives. Keep searching until you find the location that you originally had in mind when you envisioned the scenes in your head, even if you have to travel a little farther away.

   Before I shot my most recent film I made five trips to the Mojave Desert (California) in search of a location that had a natural cave that I could shoot inside for a cave scene. I bought several books about the Mojave area and scoured them for photos of any caves. I found several photos, and after some more extensive research, I set out searching for them. I located several of the caves in my first two days, but they were either too small, or too well known. Too small to fit my vision of an underground cave, or too well-traveled by tourists and Park Rangers to set up shop with my cast and crew (*Mitchell Caverns* is world-renowned).

   After scratching most of the choices off my list, I still had one more choice that I had not yet been able to locate. The picture of this cave that I saw in one of my books was really impressive, but there were no clear directions on how to find it. I visited the nearby towns and showed various people the photo of the cave, but no-one knew where it was located.

   I finally stopped in at the local visitor's center, and a very kind, grey-haired gentleman who knew that area like the back of his hand recognized the photo, and told me he had been to the cave once before a long time ago. He gave me general directions to the cave, but it took me three more trips to that area to eventually find it. I had literally walked right over the cave a couple of times on previous trips without even noticing it. My instinct and strong navigational skills told me to keep searching in that particular area though, and I finally found it on the fourth trip to the Mojave Desert.

In the end, it was worth it, for the cave was huge, and located in an area where no-one at all was around. It provided me with one of the most impressive locations of the movie, and made for a very relaxed, interesting series of film shoots that I will never forget. One time we entered the cave on a hot, sunny day, only to emerge hours later after filming to see a blanket of snow covering the surrounding desert. Of course, we took advantage of this unique incident and worked it into the storyline. My exhaustive search for this location paid off big time.

Do a little research first

Before you go out to scout a location in the wilderness you should do some research using maps of the area. These maps can typically be purchased at towns that are located nearby. Most maps will indicate if land is owned by the government (which ultimately means you, me, and every other American). Don't just go out to a wilderness location and set up shop without first knowing who owns the land. You could be asking for trouble. An irate land owner can put an end to your shoot will quickly, not to mention hurt you. You could lose more than just money from a cancelled shoot.

LOCATION SCOUTING   /   57.

If you choose a wilderness location that is not on property owned by someone you know, then try to choose one that is on public property (Federal Land, State Park, etc...). You would much rather deal with a curious Park Ranger who happens to stumble upon your shoot than you would an angry property owner. The Park Ranger is a public employee who is sworn to uphold the law, whereas the angry private property owner is sworn to keep trespassers off his land. They both can carry guns, but the property owner is more likely to use his weapon to enforce his laws.

Do not check in with the local film commission office of the nearest town for a tour of available filming locations when you go to scout a location. This will only bog down your fast-paced shooting schedule and cost you money for filming permits. Go to the visitor's center for that town instead. You will learn all there is to know about that area, and if you don't mention a word about your plans to film, no-one will tell you that you need filming permits. You are just a tourist who is sight-seeing, if anyone asks.

If you plan to shoot at a location without a permit, then plan to do it as quickly as possible. The idea is to get in, shoot quickly, and vacate the premises as soon as possible. You can gauge the urgency of the situation by the amount of people who are around or nearby the area. Whether it is a city scene, or a nature scene, you can usually shoot at least one scene in a public place and quickly be on your way before anyone from the local film commission is alerted (which rarely happens if you don't draw too much attention to yourself, and fly under the radar so to speak).

If a Park Ranger does happen to bother you when you are filming in a wilderness location without a permit, they will usually let you slide when you tell him it is your first time filming a movie and you didn't know that you needed a permit to film at that location. Plead ignorance, and tell them you are sorry. When they see how small your outfit is, they usually don't hassle you too much, as long as you are not disturbing the area in any way.

The best wilderness locations are the ones that have absolutely nobody around for miles. Just make sure there is a town with a fairly cheap (yet decent) motel close to the location so you don't have to drag your equipment and your tired cast and crew very far to their rooms at the end of a long day (and possibly night) of filming.

5

Finding a Good, Affordable Crew

Assembling a crew for your film that will work hard and for very little money is one of your most daunting tasks, and one of the most important ones that you will face on this project. The crew is the heart and soul of any film production. Unfortunately, the good ones with a lot of experience do not come cheaply, so you have to find a crew that is a diamond in the rough; a crew that is hungry (ambitious) and talented, made up of people who share your passion for filmmaking, and just haven't had a chance to shows their talents yet on a large scale. If you have a good, small, tight crew that is reliable and capable of doing hard work, your movie production experience will go smoothly. If you don't, it will be nothing but headaches from anxiety caused by such things as last minute cancellations, sub-par work, and constant arguments.

Do not hire trouble-makers

Be very careful who you choose for your crew, for your creative vision is riding on it. You do not want to put the outcome of your film in jeopardy by hiring an incompetent crew. And that means everyone. Your crew is only as strong as your weakest link. If everyone is firing away on all cylinders on a shoot except for one person who is

FINDING A GOOD, AFFORDABLE CREW   /   60.

complaining all the time, then the whole shoot is slowed down because you have to address this person's problems.

I can't express to you how important it is to enlist people that are team players, and not trouble-makers. In order to be able to make a movie with a small amount of money you have to eliminate as many foreseeable problems as possible so that all tasks take the smallest amount of time possible to execute. Problems slow you down. Trouble-makers cause problems. It is not a good idea to hire them.

A talented cinematographer with a good "demo reel" is not worth enlisting if they argue with you all the time. A soundman with all his own equipment is not worth enlisting in your crew either if he sometimes doesn't show up to work.

You really need to find out as much as you can about any potential crew members before you hire them. Just like with location scouting, you must do a character assessment of a candidate before you do business with them. Again, you are looking for people that seem like good people, not the other kind. You have to ask yourself: is this someone that I want to trust my film vision with, and spend long hours working with on various locations?

You must get to know potential crew members by setting up a meeting with them where you either have lunch with the somewhere, meet them at a park, go over to their house, or invite them to your house. If they pass the initial interview on the phone, and they have displayed talent in whatever sample of work they submitted to you, then you should set up a meeting at one of the aforementioned places

FINDING A GOOD, AFFORDABLE CREW   /   61.

so you can ask them a few questions. Basically, this meeting is for you to do a quick character assessment. It is best to do these meetings with one person at a time so you can really focus on what each particular person is all about.

In each meeting you want to ask the person the same questions you asked your actors when you were casting, such as "how do you feel about working for much less money than usual?" If they give you any kind of negative reply, stay away from them. Any hint of arrogance tells you that this person is not in it for the same reasons as you, and it is a clear sign that there might be trouble ahead if you enlist them as a crew member on your film production. On the other hand, if they say something like "I am not worried about the money on this film project because I understand the dilemma of the independent filmmaker! Man!", then you should seriously think about signing them up.

Getting along is the most important thing

When I was in my senior year of film school at CSUN (California State University, Northridge) I did a project for one of my classes that included an investigation of the main things that people in the film industry are looking for when they hire people to work for them. I thought it would be a good idea that might help me and all of my classmates find jobs in the film industry after graduating (I did a lecture, and then showed them a short film that I had made on the subject). My research included interviews with the heads of studios (or with people as close to top as possible) in which I asked them such questions as "what is the most important thing you are looking for in an employee when you hire them?" The most common answer I received was that they are looking for people that they can get along with.

Tex Rudloff, the head of Lions Gate Studios at that time told me in an interview that getting along with people is by far the most important thing that he considers before he hires a person to work for him. He said "a person could have all the talent in the world, but if I can't get along with them, I don't want to work with them."

Nobody wants to work with a difficult person. Choose your crew wisely, surround yourself with good people who are as passionate about making your film as you are, and you will be happy with the results, for not only will your film be created on a meager budget, but you will also have a very good time during the process.

It is not easy to get film industry crew people to work for the amount of money you are offering. Anyone who has any real experience is used to being paid serious money for the work they do, and this makes it difficult for you to compete with when all you are offering is "peanuts" for pay. Unless you have a close relative who is a professional cinematographer and agrees to help you out on weekends, or you get very lucking with your search, you will not be able to afford an experienced DP/Cinematographer.

What you need to do is find people who have a little experience in the film industry, and want more experience badly. There are a lot of very talented cinematographers, soundmen, props people, etc..., who are just dying to put their talents and equipment to use, even if it means working for a lot less pay than the industry standard. It is the same phenomenon as the one I mentioned in the section about finding actors in that it is very competitive (but not quite as bad).

  Like I said earlier, it is feast or famine in the film industry, and this applies to crew members as well. People will be willing to make deals with you to work for very little money just to keep working and creating, not to mention learning. Most of these people have invested a lot of money in expensive equipment as well, and they must keep working in any way to pay for it. Your little movie is not as small as you think to people who badly need movies to work on. Do not underestimate how important your efforts are to certain other people.

  Do not forget the importance of having creative control either. This works the same with crew members as it does with actors, or anyone else working on a small film. Tell them that they will be able to perform their job without the hands of big business being involved, and this will make your job offer seem more attractive. This only means more creative control for them. Creative control is very important to creative types.

  Everyone who works in the film industry wants the freedom to apply their talent without someone breathing down their neck and telling them how to do it. Many famous filmmakers have said that they often look back on the beginning of their career and say that it was the most enjoyable time of their lives. This is when the artist has the most freedom. An artist must have freedom to create and express themselves in order for them to thrive. Without this freedom, artists become frustrated, and unhappy.

FINDING A GOOD, AFFORDABLE CREW   /   64.

   The thing that makes your film project so appealing to those who work in the film industry is that you are offering them creative control. Your production is cut down to the bare bones and offers the art of film in its raw form, ready to be made into a movie by the artists who get their hands on it. You are essentially offering creative freedom to those who will agree to work for very little pay. Remember, you are the one who has organized and funded this film project, and you are essentially providing a canvas for film industry artists to work on, so don't think that you have to beg people to work on your film.

Go straight to the source

   There are several different ways to find good, affordable crew people. One of the best ways that I have found to find 16mm cinematographers with their own camera packages as well as sound people with their own sound recording packages is to go to places that rent this kind of equipment and hang out for a while. By hang out, I mean go in and talk to the people at the counter, as well as anyone else who seems friendly that is there picking up film industry equipment packages.

   The first thing you want to do is find the places near you that rent equipment to film industry people. Do a keyword search on the internet for *film industry equipment rental* along with the name of the largest city nearest to where you live. Another way to find them is to look in the yellow pages of any large city near you. Look under *film industry equipment, camera rental, sound equipment rental,* or even *equipment rental.* You can also find places that rent film industry equipment by asking the person at the newsstand (where you go to buy your actor's trade magazine) if they sell *American Cinematographer* or *American Film* magazines. There are ads for film industry equipment rental houses in both of these magazines.

When you go in to the rental houses, tell the people at the counter that you are making a movie with your own paychecks and you want to know how much it would cost to rent equipment from them. This way you have established that you are an independent filmmaker who works on a very small budget, and they might give you a deal if you ever do rent equipment from them. I will explain next why they would be willing to do this, but trust me, if you tell these people you are making a movie, they will welcome you, despite your lack of major funding.

Although you are not one of the biggest customers an equipment rental house could hope to find, and you will not bring much money in to them at the present time, these guys understand the importance of growing with a customer. As your career grows, you will have more money available to rent larger, more expensive packages. They know that if you start out with them, and you are treated right, you will probably stick with them throughout your career. This means more money for everyone involved. Believe me, the people who work at film industry equipment rental houses are just as anxious as you are to see your career take off.

While you are waiting to be helped take notice of the people who are picking up equipment. Tell them about your film and try to talk to them about their project (if they seem nice enough to approach). People in the film industry

FINDING A GOOD, AFFORDABLE CREW   /   66.

usually like to talk about the projects they are working on. Whether it is to brag, or just to make conversation, that's just how it is.

You can learn a lot about a person's career just by talking to them at these equipment rental houses. Through these conversations you should ask these people if they have a 16mm camera package (or for sound, a DAT recorder package) of their own. If they do, you want to immediately tell them the short version of your script and how you are looking for people that would be willing to work cheaply (in exchange for having creative control).

You can appeal to their plan

Most professional Directors of Photography and cameramen have their own 16mm camera packages. They all started their careers using this type of camera, and they may still have their old package hanging around in their closet. Some of them have been working for a long time in the film industry, and may have become cynical. The corporate control and commercialism aspects of their jobs have them longing for the days when no-one stifled their creative visions, hindered their creative plans, or told them how to create their art. Some of these people have been dreaming of working on an independent film to get back to their roots. Many of the crew people who are currently working in the film industry desire to return to the days when filmmaking was less complicated, and more honest.

Believe it or not, you and your small film are just the thing some very experienced, yet frustrated crew people are

FINDING A GOOD, AFFORDABLE CREW / 67.

looking for to restore their faith in the art of film. Your project gives them a chance to break out their old, trusty 16mm camera package (that made them who they are today) and get back to the basics of creating art on film. The same goes for sound people, prop masters, special effects people, and anyone else who works as crew in the film industry.

No matter what your job is in this business, the more successful you are the more complicated your job gets. Don't be afraid to make conversation with the people at equipment rental houses, for chances are they are looking for people like you. You may be their ticket back to the good old days when they had more control and fewer restrictions. They all just want creative freedom, and you can offer it to them.

It is also a good idea to tell the people behind the rental counter all about your movie production plans. A lot of these people are camera or sound people that used to work on movies but fell on hard times and were forced to take a "real" job behind a counter. Some of these people own their own equipment packages and would like nothing better than to work on a movie again (on their day off, of course). Don't worry about annoying them, for you are a potential customer of theirs and this will spare you the bum's rush out the door when you start asking a lot of questions.

Before you leave any equipment rental house you should ask one of the people you talk to if you can leave a small stack of business cards on a corner of the counter or a few pinned to their bulletin board. On the business cards write "DP/Cinematographer (or for audio places: Soundman)

FINDING A GOOD, AFFORDABLE CREW / 68.

wanted for low budget film". You should get some decent replies.

Another way to find good, affordable crew members is to post ads on film industry web sites. These ads should include:

1. The headline: CREW MEMBERS WANTED FOR LOW BUDGET MOVIE.

2. A list of the crew positions you are looking to fill, along with the job descriptions.

3. The following words at the end:
VHS/DVD copy of film and SOME PAY.

4. Also at the end of the ad include the words: Send resume and reel.

5. Your email and address (using a P.O. box is advised).

Websites where you can place an ad to find good, affordable crew members:

- http://www.mandy.com/

- http://www.filmstew.com/

- http://www.gigslist.org/resumes/

- http://www.thedailycall.com/

FINDING A GOOD, AFFORDABLE CREW   /   69.

    When you are negotiating with potential crew members, be sure to stress the creative control aspect. This is your best bargaining chip. Tell them that you are producing and directing the film, but they are in charge of their job. You will not bother them as long as they portray *your* vision accurately. If they are hungry to work (like with actors) they will be willing to lower their usual rate substantially in return for creative control. The difference is that the kind of crew members you are looking for offer equipment along with their labor deal (16mm camera packages, sound equipment, etc...) so you are essentially paying for their specialized labor, and the rental of their equipment. You have to pay the ones who bring their own equipment a little more than the other people in the movie.

    The equipment thing is a big deal, for it will save you thousands of dollars in equipment rental and insurance fees. The insurance fees on a camera package alone will cost you over $200 a day! If you must rent equipment yourself, the best thing to do about insurance is to find an insurance company that specializes in "short-term" insurance for film industry equipment rental. It is expensive, but mandatory for any film equipment package rentals.

Websites that offer information about insurance for film industry equipment:

- http://www.aeinsurance.com/

- http://www.amvfproductions.com/insurance.html

- http://www.productioninsurance.com/

FINDING A GOOD, AFFORDABLE CREW / 70.

The thing that you are striving to achieve with the assembly of your crew is a "run and gun" outfit that works fast, yet with quality. You want people that understand that time is money for you, and you cannot afford to waste any of it. You want a crew that can descend upon a city street (or any location), set up their equipment almost on the fly, shoot and record, pack up quickly, and then depart the area before a crowd gathers. You must work with an understanding that you are circumventing the Hollywood system with the way that you are making your movie, and the usual rules of a standard film production do not apply. You are working underground so to speak, and not quite out in the open. Not illegal, just not quite playing by the rules.

There is no need to worry too much about film commissions and permits if you can shoot your scenes fast, without too much technical set-up, and with a small amount of people. Keep it really small and don't draw any attention to yourself, and nobody will bother you. You will be in and out of most public locations before the local film commission gets wind of you. More than likely, they never will.

Any actors that might be involved in one of these quick shoots need to rehearse their parts thoroughly in another location (like at a park) ahead of time so there is no need to rehearse on the scene of a public shoot. The same goes with any crew set-ups. If you are shooting at a wilderness location where no-one else is around, then you have the luxury to rehearse right on the set, but when you are shooting in any public place, rehearse ahead of time to reduce your time at that location.

FINDING A GOOD, AFFORDABLE CREW   /   71.

A crew meeting will be held before every shoot to discuss all the requirements for each scene regarding camera, sound, props, etc... Any blocking or difficult set-ups should be practiced during these meetings so that everyone knows what is expected of them on each particular shoot. Any research from your location scout should be shared with your crew at these meetings. Show them your notes and photos so that they can get an idea of what they might need to get their jobs done. Due diligence and thorough pre-production of a location are the keys to getting in and out of a location quickly, yet with good results.

You must never ask for a *freebie*

One thing I suggest you never do is ask anyone to work on your movie for free. Whether it be a starving actor, or a potential crew member who seems so nice that you think they wouldn't mind working for free, never ask them to do it. Trust me on this one Pay everyone something, even if it is much less than they are used to getting paid for their job.

First of all, if you are paying the people who work on your movie something, no matter how small, then they are officially *working* for you. If you pay them nothing for their services, then they are basically doing you a favor. When there is absolutely no monetary connection to the job you are asking them to perform they can pretty much abandon you at any time if they don't like how the production is going (for whatever reason). Of course, they can do this even if you pay them, but they are much less likely to do so if there is any kind of money involved no matter how small. It is just something about the thought of working for free. People really hate working for free. If you

FINDING A GOOD, AFFORDABLE CREW   /   72.

ask them to work without pay, there is a good chance that they will not give you a 100% effort and they could abandon you when things get tough on your production.

As I stated earlier; your crew should be small, tight, and fast on their feet. You have to stress to everyone who works on your movie that everyone is expected to work at a faster than normal pace. Explain to everyone that the success of your production depends upon getting the movie "in the can" as quickly as possible. Also, everyone has to agree to do more than one job, and not complain about it.

The usual luxuries that are afforded to movies with big budgets do not exist on your production (due to your budget constraints). There is no "hurry up and wait" on your film production where cast and crew stand around on your dollar while you wait for some guy to rig a light. Instead, it is "hurry up and don't ever wait". The idea is to become a well-oiled machine that clicks on all cylinders and cranks out scenes like a production line, with NO DOWN TIME.

The crew on a movie that is shot with a very, very low budget should be as small as you can possibly get away with and still get your scenes shot. There is no caterer, make-up person, or personal assistants of any kind. Lunches should be "brown-bagged". Actors will do their own make-up. Everyone will be expected to do stuff that is not part of their usual job description. Once again, everyone must understand that getting the movie made is more important than how much money they are getting paid.

FINDING A GOOD, AFFORDABLE CREW   /   73.

You should include the following positions in your bare-bones, "run and gun" crew:

PRODUCER/DIRECTOR/(WRITER)- This is you.

Payment:

Your **payment comes when your film is completed and you sell it to a distribution company.**

You are not only the producer, director, and (possibly) writer on your film, but you are also the Art Director, Costume/Props person, caterer, grip, etc... You are the backbone of the entire film production. Like I said earlier, making a movie with a very, very low budget requires passion and commitment, and you must sustain a high level of both to succeed. YOU are where the buck stops with everything on your movie. You must do more jobs than anyone could reasonably expect one person to do if you want good results. One minute you are the caterer who is putting out sandwiches for lunch, the next minute you are in a deep discussion with one of your actors about a heavy scene you are about to direct. You must have a very positive attitude, strong motivational skills, and an ironclad resolve to get your film made, no matter what it takes (as long as it is legal and ethically sound). You must know the basics of film production yet you must practice extraordinary methods sometimes to get the job done.

- **DIRECTOR OF PHOTOGRAPHY/CINEMATOGRAPHER/GRIP-**

Payment:

1. $200/day.

2. Film title and credit.

3. A VHS/DVD copy of your film.

    This person should provide their own 16mm "crystal sync" (sound) camera package, lenses, and a "focus puller" camera assistant (that you will pay separately). They are expected to take care of all the things that are necessary to run the camera, film your movie, change the film, and hand the nicely labeled cans of 16mm film over to you at the end of each shoot. The "look" of your film has a lot to do with the DP, so make sure you choose someone with an impressive "reel". Whoever does this job is also in charge of getting the camera equipment in and out of any scenes you shoot. They have to be willing to do grip work, rigging, and lighting, as well as any other tasks that might be required to get any shots. They also have to be willing to work long, hard hours (like everyone else you hire).

- **FOCUS PULLER/CAMERA ASSISTANT/GRIP-**

Payment:

1. $75/day.

2. Film title and credit.

3. A VHS/DVD copy of your film.

FINDING A GOOD, AFFORDABLE CREW   /   75.

   This person is the DP/Cinematographer/Grip's "right hand man", and should be chosen by that person to do that job. A certain degree of familiarity with each other's work style is a major factor in how smoothly the filming will go. Besides "pulling focus", this person is in charge of anything that has to do with helping the DP/Cinematographer/Grip set up their equipment and get their shots. Carrying camera equipment, labeling film cans, setting up lights, and holding reflectors are some of the other responsibilities that come with this position.

- **SOUNDMAN (PERSON)/GRIP-**

Payment:

   1. $150/day.

   2. Film title and credit.

   3. A VHS/DVD copy of your film.

   The person that you hire for this position must have their own portable DAT recorder (digital audio tape recorder) package that includes time-code and a digital slate, as well as a "boom" microphone, walkie-talkies, and several "wireless" microphones. This person is responsible for setting up sound equipment and recording the audio of your scenes. At the end of every shoot they will hand over to you the nicely labeled DAT tapes (with log sheets). They should also be able to refer you to a "boom operator" audio assistant that you can hire to help them with any tasks involved with recording the audio of your scenes.

FINDING A GOOD, AFFORDABLE CREW   /   76.

- **BOOM OPERATOR/AUDIO ASSISTANT/GRIP-**

Payment:

   1. $75/day.

   2. Film title and credit.

   3. A VHS/DVD copy of your film.

The person who does this job is responsible for doing such things as placing the "boom" microphone in the best positions of every shot for recording audio (off camera), setting up wireless microphones that can be heard but not seen by the camera when used by actors, labeling DAT (digital audio) tapes, as well as carrying and helping the soundman set up any sound equipment. He is basically expected to do what ever it takes to help the soundman get the best quality sound recordings of every scene you shoot during your film production.

- **ASSISTANT DIRECTOR/PRODUCTION MANAGER/GRIP-**

Payment:

   1. $75/day.

   2. Film title and credit.

   3. A VHS/DVD copy of your film.

FINDING A GOOD, AFFORDABLE CREW / 77.

While this crew member is not bringing any expensive equipment when you hire them, their job is just as important as any of the other ones on your production. The person that you hire for this position must bring strong managerial and organizational skills with them every day they come to work. They are in charge of such things as rallying your troops when it comes time to film, getting actors to show up on the set and hit their mark, making sure the necessary props, furniture, and equipment are all in place for each scene, and telling people to be quiet before the filming begins.

The person you hire for this position must know what is expected from everyone on the set, and make sure that they all do their job. The AD/Production Manager/Grip must be able to bring people together, and get things done under difficult circumstances. They must be even-tempered and adept at dealing with the different personalities of the actors and crew members on your film. This person is basically in charge of doing the managerial heavy lifting, so that you, the Producer/Director/Writer can focus as much as possible on doing the creative stuff. If your film production were a ship, then you would be the captain, and the AD/Production Manager/Grip would be your first mate.

This person must be disciplined in their work ethic, and willing to confront any actors or crew members who are not doing what they are supposed to be doing. You are paying this person to keep everyone in line, and get them to give you the best possible work effort they have to offer. Whomever you hire for this position will be your second in command on any set and will be responsible for keeping your well-oiled film production machine running smoothly.

FINDING A GOOD, AFFORDABLE CREW   /   78.

Choose this person very carefully, for they have a lot of responsibilities, and the quality of your film could depend on this decision.

• **SCRIPT SUPERVISOR/PRODUCTION ASSISTANT/GRIP-**

Payment:

   1. $50/day.

   2. Film title and credit.

   3. A VHS/DVD copy of your film.

The person who does this job is responsible for making sure that your film production effort yields a product that is faithful to your script. This individual is the guardian of your film vision. A copy of the script must be with them at all times. They must refer to it constantly, and remind people that accuracy and continuity are important. They must monitor every detail of every shoot and step in when necessary to correct anyone who strays from your creative vision. From little things like telling actors to remove wrist watches for scenes that are set far in the past, to bigger things like telling the DP/Cinematographer/Grip that they can't shoot a scene because the sun is high in the sky, and the script calls for a scene that takes place at sunrise, the Script Supervisor/Production Assistant must be a constant defender of the details in your story and an administrator of your storyline. Other duties include getting scripts and "sides" to the actors, as well as organizing and managing rehearsals. This person is also expected to be a multi-

FINDING A GOOD, AFFORDABLE CREW   /   79.

purpose production assistant that will perform various tasks to help keep the production running smoothly, such as helping to set up meals and carrying stuff. They will also be the one who runs any errands that are necessary while on location. When they are not hounding people to stay loyal to the script this person will help out in any way that is necessary to get things moving along when you are shooting.

- **PROPS/COSTUME/ SPECIAL EFFECTS PERSON-**

Payment:

   1. $50/day.

   2. Film title and credit.

   3. A VHS/DVD copy of your film.

The main job of the Pops/Costume/Special Effects person is to distribute and maintain all of the props, costumes and special effects materials that are involved with the production of your movie. You will be providing them with all of the items involved with props, costumes, and special effects so that you will not have to pay to have them made. This will save you a lot of money. I will explain how to find good props and costumes literally for pennies in another section. Your well written low budget script does not require a lot of expensive props and costumes, so this person will actually need to be more of a grip than a props person or a costume designer. Occasionally this person may have to fix a costume or create a basic prop on the set, so they should bring a small sewing kit and a full set of tools with them every day when they come to work. This person will also be in charge of doing any special effects make-up. You will supply the materials for these types of things as well.

What I have described here is my list of the necessary crew you will need if you want to have a "run and gun" crew that is fast on their feet. I suggest that you limit your crew to no more than eight people, including yourself. Besides the fact that you cannot afford to employ any more people, it is not a good idea to have a crew that is any bigger than the one I described above. You should bring no more than fifteen people when you show up to film at a location, and that includes your actors. The less people you have, the faster, and stealthier you will be when you are shooting. You do not want to attract any crowds anywhere you are shooting. You need to get in, shoot your scene, and then get out quickly. A small crew is necessary for this type of filming.

Here is a recap of the list of 8 suggested crew members:

- **PRODUCER/DIRECTOR/WRITER (yourself)**

- **DIRECTOR OF PHOTOGRAPHY/CINEMATOGRAPHER/GRIP**

- **FOCUS PULLER/CAMERA ASSISTANT/GRIP**

- **SOUNDMAN (PERSON)/GRIP**

- **BOOM OPERATOR/AUDIO ASSISTANT/GRIP**

- **ASSISTANT DIRECTOR/PRODUCTION MANAGER/GRIP**

- **SCRIPT SUPERVISOR/PRODUCTION ASSISTANT/GRIP**

- **PROPS/COSTUME PERSON/GRIP**

Take your time and make sure that you find the right crew people for your film production. In this case, the right people means those who are talented, skilled, easy to work with, responsible, hard working, and willing to work for very little pay. I have had some very good experiences working with crew members on my films, but I have also had some very bad ones. Your dream is not something you want to trust in the hands of anyone who does not meet the requirements that I have just described. There are people out there who will meet those requirements, and they are anxious to get to work on your film. All you need to do is a little research, and you will find them.

6

Pre-Production

This stage of your film production process should not be taken lightly. If you do the proper amount of pre-production work on your film you will be able to save a lot of money throughout the entire process. This is due to the fact that you have the opportunity to scrutinize every aspect of the production requirements and eliminate foreseeable problems that slow you down and cost you money. If you have everything ready, things tend to move right along when you are filming. If you do not do an ample amount of pre-production for your film you are destined to run into problems every step of the way that will ultimately cost you time and eat up your small budget rather quickly.

Pre-production is the part where you do your homework and get everything prepared for the big test so to speak (when filming begins). This is the phase of your project when you do research and set-up everything that is necessary to make your film shoots go quickly, and with good results.

Your pre-production process actually begins when you acquire your script and secure the budget to make it into a film. However, the real work begins when you do your location scouting, choose your cast, and hire your crew. Since I have already devoted a chapter to each one of the aforementioned pre-production duties, I will concentrate on the remaining ones in this section.

• **BUDGET BREAKDOWN-**

This is the part where you add up all the things in your film production that are going to cost you money, and decide how much of your budget will be devoted to each one.

FISCAL RESPONSIBILITY IS REQUIRED if you ever want your film to see the light of day (or the light of a movie screen). You must be very strict with your spending limits on every aspect of your film.

A separate bank account is a good idea

You should open a bank account that is separate from the one you have to pay your personal bills and use it solely to pay for products and services related to the production of your film. This will assure that your film budget will not be eaten up accidentally by some unforeseen financial problem that may come up in your life.

This is my basic Budget Breakdown for a film with a $50,000 budget (using your own script and storyboard):

16mm FILM STOCK AND FILM RELATED SERVICES (lab processing fees, work print, final print, etc...)- $15,000

CREW (based on a 15 day shooting schedule with the 7 stated crew members, using my pay scale for crew)- $10,125

CAST (based on a cast that has 6 principal actors, 3 supporting actors, and 3 extras working for 15 days, using my pay scale for actors that I mentioned earlier)- $9,000

TRAVEL EXPENSES (motels/hotels, gas, food, etc... for 15 people for six days of shooting) - $5,000

PROPS AND COSTUMES- $375

POST PRODUCTION (color timing, negative cutting, sound design/mixing, music, titles, etc...)- $10,500

Total-

$50,000

When you are doing your budget breakdown you can adjust each number slightly higher or lower depending on how many people are in your cast, how many days you plan to travel, etc... However, once you have finished your budget breakdown, you must be diligent in paying the allotted amount for each category. You will probably be considered a "cheapskate" by everyone you employ, but you must stay true to your budget breakdown throughout your film production. You must try to eliminate unexpected charges by thoroughly planning everything ahead of time.

• STORYBOARDING-

Your storyboard is basically a visual map that includes technical instructions for every scene in your film. In addition to the drawings you also have notes that are related to any movement, action, important camera angles, etc... It is the first step in the process of bringing your film vision off the paper and into a visual form that includes images instead of just words. It is the first step of a long technical process that will ultimately result in a film product.

A copy of your storyboard should be given to all the members of your cast and crew. You do not need to include actor's dialogue in a storyboard (except in certain circumstances that I will explain about later). That is why actors have a copy of the script. Your cast will benefit from the storyboard mainly because they can learn about what is expected from them in terms of blocking, movement, etc... Your storyboard will help you (and your cast and crew) better understand the technical things that are required to film the scenes of your movie. It is much more a technical layout than an artistic display. You do not need to have an artistic drawing ability to make a storyboard. It doesn't hurt if you were a cartoonist your whole life, but illustration talent is not required. Also, there are computer programs available that make it easy for anyone to draw a storyboard.

In the end; if you do your own storyboard, you will understand better everything in your film production that

PRE-PRODUCTION   /   86.

needs to be done in terms of blocking, camera angles, movement, etc... You will also save some money by not having to pay a storyboard artist and that money can be used to pay for the most important thing in your budget break-down; film stock (and the associated costs for film lab processing).

I have always done my own story boards for my movies. Not only because it saves money, but also because I was born with a talent for cartooning. I have always enjoyed drawing of any kind since I was able to hold a pencil in my hand. Storyboarding for me is a chance to draw, and that is the fun part of this process for me.

The technical aspect of storyboarding requires a little more mechanical thought than it does creativity. You must draw things and describe them in a technical way so that everyone from the cast and crew understands what they need to do before they show up at any location.

To begin the storyboarding process you need to take out all the photos and notes of the locations that you took when you did your location scouting. You will be using these as references; each frame of your storyboard must be drawn using the photo and notes that pertain to the specific location you are depicting. In the captions below each storyboard frame write down any important notes related to movement or action. Next, draw the scene as close to the photo as possible. The best way to do this is to put the photo of the location behind the storyboard paper and trace the general outlines (use thin paper when you print copies from your storyboard template). You are only trying to illustrate the general dimensions of the setting as well as the location of actors and important objects. Again, you are not trying to impress anyone with your drawing ability; you are just providing technical instructions to your cast and crew.

Each time you finish a frame of your storyboard, take the photo you used as a reference and tape it behind the frame so you will have it at the ready to show your cast and crew during pre-production meetings. This will help familiarize them with the location before they go there. It will also help you to be more accurate with the details of your instructions.

Creating a storyboard for your movie requires you to transfer your film vision from the written word to a series of drawings that depicts every shot for every scene in your film. It is a map of your film that will be used by everyone in your cast and crew to get an idea of what you want your movie to look like. As the Producer/Director of your movie it is your responsibility to determine how this map is drawn.

Deciding on the different shots of your movie requires creative vision and strong directorial skills. You must picture your movie in your head throughout the entire process while at the same time staying aware of technical requirements.

Draw each frame of your storyboard as if you were sitting in front of a screen and watching a slide show of every shot of your film. Think of the words you write in the captions below as the commentary you must provide to explain to your cast and crew what is happening in each slide. You must be very diligent on this task and think very hard about the things they might need to know in order to understand what you need from them when the filming begins.

Keep it simple

Keep your technical requirements simple and easy to execute. For instance; do not require a camera angle that must crane down from the top of a building then zoom in through a window and end up on a close-up of your main character, which then begins talking. That kind of shot requires a lot of money and time to prepare and execute. Besides that, it carries with it a large margin for error. You could spend all day and ten rolls of film on that shot and still not get it right. Obviously, you can't afford that when you are working with a small budget. A lot of people who direct movies want to be Orson Welles, but the reality of it is; even if you have the talent you need a big budget to make a movie with the stylized camera moves of *Citizen Kane (1941)*. Be creative, but make it simple to execute.

Important things only

Write down only your most important notes in the captions below the storyboard frames. For example; if a character enters the scene, something happens in the background that is important, or an important piece of action occurs, write it down. Do not write down things like character dialogue unless it pertains to something the crew is involved with, such as a character quickly turning to the camera to say something in which the DP/Cinematographer/Grip must zoom in on their face.

Do not over produce any scene for it will only send you over your budget quickly. Again, try to make things simple yet creative. For example; a furniture dolly or a wheel chair will work just fine for a moving dolly shot instead of a time consuming and labor intensive tracking shot. Moving a camera person on a wheelchair through a crowd of people is a lot easier than laying down tracks on a public street.

When you make a movie with a very, very, low budget, you do not have the luxury of using more than one camera. This is actually a benefit when it comes to the storyboard for there are fewer frames to draw. There is no "second unit" crew with a small production. You, your crew, and your *one* camera package is all you have, but it is more than enough if you are clever with your methods of production.

Most of the frames you draw should be full shots (wide shots), unless it is a close-up that is crucial to your storyline. This is because you will be shooting with a style in which you start every scene with a master shot and shoot close ups and inserts at the end (as needed). Your DP/Cinematographer/Grip should be encouraged to shoot with a "handheld" style (Steadycam, if possible) so that you will have a *cinema verite* feel to your movie where the camera seems to be a character in the film that is mingling amongst the other characters. This kind of shooting style is much faster than the static style in which every shot is planned out in advance. I will explain more about this in pages to come when I talk about directing your film.

You do not have to draw the frames of your storyboard with the kind of details that you see in some of the professional ones out there. Focus on depicting the scenes in a technical aspect. You can even draw stick figures as long as they are placed in the right locations and they indicate the right information in terms of movement, direction, etc...

Write down notes for things such as actor's positions, camera angles, as well as any kind of prop or set involvement in the scene. Any important sound or grip labor instructions should also be included.

You should draw each frame with the specific layout and camera angle that you plan to set up for that scene when you are shooting it with your cast and crew. Draw each frame the way you want to eventually see it on the screen, and then fill in the information that you think your cast and crew will need to make it happen.

The process of making a film requires you to move your film vision from your head, to the script pages, to the storyboard pages, to the film stock, and then finally, to the screen. Each one of these steps are equally important, so make sure you devote as much effort to storyboarding as you do to the other steps of your film production.

All films begin with a creative thought which then requires a series of labor events to bring it to life. Once you have your idea you must add to it the necessary technical assignments needed to make it into a film. Think of the storyboard as just another step in the technical process of producing a film.

PRE-PRODUCTION / 91.

Do not be intimidated by the creative appearance of some of the professional storyboards you may see on the internet at various storyboard websites. A pretty storyboard is nice, but it is not mandatory. If you can draw a stick person, then you can make your own storyboard and save yourself a lot of money.

Websites that offer information and software for drawing storyboards:

- http://www.thestoryboardartist.com/tutorial.html

- http://www.storyboardartist.com/artist.html

- http://www.exposure.co.uk/eejit/storybd/

- http://www.filmmakerstore.com/stbdart.htm

If you do not want to do your own storyboarding, then you can hire a storyboard artist to do it for you. As with your cast and crew, look for talented people that are hungry to work. There are plenty of them out there and most of them will give you a good price for their work. If you feel that you would spend more time than it is worth doing your own storyboard and you have a little bit of extra budget money set aside for your storyboard, then it might be a good idea to hire one of these storyboard artists. Just make sure you work closely with them to ensure that your vision is depicted correctly on the frames they draw.

Websites that offer information on finding storyboard artists for hire:

- http://www.frameworks-la.com/home_page.html

- http://www.foregroundimage.com/motion/2D_animation.asp?ggkey=storyboard+artist

- http://folioplanet.com/Illustration/Storyboards/

When your storyboard is finished, make enough copies to distribute it to everyone in your cast and crew.

• SCRIPT BREAKDOWN-

Making a script breakdown is the tedious yet necessary process of going through every page of your script and identifying the physical objects for each scene of your movie that you will need to film it. Sets, props, costumes, furniture, etc... All these things need to be acquired by you and the first step in doing so is making a script breakdown.

Once again, your low budget movie script should not have a lot of the above mentioned items in it's scenes if you expect to get your film made with very little money.

The best way to do the script breakdown is to use 4 different colored "highlighter" pens to mark the 4 different types of things you are looking for in each scene. It does not matter what colors you choose. For this explanation I will use yellow, pink, green, and blue. Yellow will represent the set you will be using for a scene. Pink will be for any furniture required. Green will be for costumes, and blue will be for props.

PRE-PRODUCTION   /   93.

Start by numbering each scene in your script (starting with scene #1). Next, write down each scene number on a blank page, one page for each number. After that you want to go through your script one scene at a time and highlight all the physical things you need to make it look on film the way it reads in your script.

Use the **yellow pen** first to highlight the **heading** of each scene in your script (IE: EXT. COUNTRY ROAD DAY). The purpose of this is to identify the location where you will film the scene at, as well as any sets that need to be built for that scene. Of course, your set building must be kept to a minimum on a film with a small budget, so this is mainly just to identify the location. After that, write down each scene heading that you just highlighted on the corresponding blank pages that you numbered. Highlight them in yellow as you did in your script. Next, write below each heading on each page any set building that is required. If it is a wilderness location or one that requires no set building just write the word "NONE" below the heading.

The next step is to take your **pink pen** and highlight all the **furniture** that is required in each scene. Make a list of the furniture in each scene and then write each list on the corresponding scene pages where you just put the headings. Write each list below the header information and then highlight it in pink.

Repeat the same process using the **green pen** for all the **costumes** and then repeat the same process using the **blue pen** for all the **props** in each scene. Put the lists of each below the furniture list on each scene page, and highlight them with their respective colors.

Each one of these pages represents a scene in your movie, and every physical item you will need to film it. This is your basic script breakdown and you can refer to it when you are acquiring the stuff you need for each scene. You can also refer to it when you are setting up to film a scene. Your AD/Production Manager/Grip will need a copy of this on every shoot for he is in charge of getting everything set up and ready to film.

• MAKING A SHOOTING SCHEDULE-

A well-planned shooting schedule is a major factor in saving you money on a low budget film production. This stage of your project must be done with the idea in mind that *speed* and *efficiency* save you money. How quickly can you get your film" in the can" while still creating a quality product is the name of the game. The smaller the number of your shooting days, the smaller the amount of money you will have to take from your budget to pay your cast and crew.

Remember, film stock and lab fees are expensive, and most of your budget should be devoted to those costs. You cannot negotiate prices with Kodak, or any quality film lab. You really have no control over the price this aspect of your film. Unless you are still a *student* and you can show a student ID, then you can get about a 10-20% discount.

You get no breaks on film costs once you become a *professional* filmmaker. You just have to pay the prices that the rest of the film industry people pay when it comes to film and lab fees. There are other things however that you can control a little more, and this is where you can save money.

The shooting schedule is something that you have a good amount of control over (along with many other things) with your film production. You can save a lot of money if you do it the right way.

The first thing you need to do is make a **list** of all the **shots** of your movie that you have in your storyboard and **assign a number** to each one.

Next, **break down** your shot list **by location** into several smaller lists, with each list representing all the shots that take place at a certain location. When you are done with this step you will basically have a bunch of lists that represent all the locations of your film with all the shots you need to film at each location.

For the next step you need to figure **how long** each **individual shot** on all of your location shot lists will take to shoot. This is where your knowledge of film production and the level of faith you have in your crew come into play.

Look at each shot and take into consideration the difficulty factors involved in shooting it, then estimate how much time it will take for you to get it done. Write the estimated time next to each shot.

After that, tally up the **total time** for **each list**. Write your totals at the bottom of each list with a number that represents total working hours required to shoot all of the shots on that list (not including travel time).

Divide each total number of hours **by 10** (your average number of hours you expect everyone to work) and this will give you the **total number of days** you need to spend shooting at each location.

Write the total number of days at the bottom of each list.

Add up all the days at the bottom of each list and write it at the bottom of the last page. This is your **total number of shooting days** required to get your film "in the can".

If you wrote your script properly with a minimal amount of different locations for all of your scenes then your number TOTAL SHOULD BE NO MORE THAN **15 SHOOTING DAYS**. You should be able to shoot your (very) low budget feature film in 12-15 days. If you feel that you cannot do it in this amount of time then you need to change some things in your script that will make your production less complicated.

The next thing you need to do is **assign shooting days** to **each location** shot list. Before you do this, **divide** your lists **into two groups**: locations that **require travel** arrangements, and locations that **do not require travel** arrangements.

Next, you want to take your group of location shot lists that do not require travel arrangements and schedule them to be shot first. It is better to shoot these locations first because you can see how each person works and eliminate any problematic people before you commit to a road trip with them.

Long, hard work days should be expected

For daytime shoots your work day should begin at 7:00 AM and end at 6:00 PM. If you need a sunrise shot or a scene that takes place at "golden hour", then you can shift your call time to an earlier or later start, but make sure that everyone agrees that on any given day they may be required to work the full 11 hours if necessary. Lunch breaks should be flexible in terms of how much time (30 minutes to 1 hour), and also in terms of when they are taken.

Your working hours for night time shoots should begin 1 hour before dark and end either 10 hours later, or when the filming is done, whichever comes first. Dinner breaks should be flexible in the same way as lunch breaks.

Shoot in consecutive days

Schedule your shoots so that you film on as many consecutive days as you can possibly get everyone in your cast and crew to all agree upon. Getting everyone to agree on the schedule is a constant battle. Try to get your cast and crew to commit to work at least 6 or 7 days in a row if you can. This will help you to get your film shot as quickly as possible.

Strike while the iron is hot

Plan to start shooting no more than one week after everyone agrees on the dates. The sooner you start the better. If you wait too long to start filming, some job that pays more money than yours might come along and steal some of your employees away from you.

The same scheduling rule applies to your location shot lists that require traveling and hotel accommodations. Try to get everyone to commit to as many days as possible in one trip. If you can, try to film all of these location shot lists in one week. Make sure you stay at each location as long as it takes to shoot every shot on the list. Do not count on returning to that location on another trip. This will cost you more time and money than you have to organize. Stay as many days as it takes, but shoot quickly then move on to the next location, and then return home.

Film things fast and all together

You should schedule your location shoots so that you can film all the shots on as many location lists as you can in the shortest amount of time possible. You will have to pay for your cast and crew's travel expenses, so the idea is to spend as little time possible traveling and as much time possible filming. You should not schedule any locations that are far apart from each other, for this requires a lot of travel time between shoots.

Once you get your cast and crew out on the road you want to get as much done as possible, so you do not have to organize another trip and line everything up again. You never know what can come up in the lives of your cast and crew that could prevent them from doing another location shoot, so get as much filmed as you can in one trip.

Remember to plan your film location shoots so that your different locations on the shooting schedule are as close to each other as possible. This is something that you should have taken into consideration when you where choosing your locations. If you can finish shooting one location, then pack up and move on to the next location quickly, you will be able to get a lot of shots filmed in a relatively small amount of time. This of course will get your film "in the can" faster and save you a lot of money.

Shoot in sequence

Almost every movie that you see in the major theaters is filmed "out of sequence". What this means is that the scenes are not shot in the order that the script indicates. They are not filmed in the linear order that the audience will see on the screen, but rather they are shot in whatever order the producers of the film decide they would like it filmed. With most films the shooting order of scenes is determined by many different factors such as script requirements regarding weather, location availability, actor's schedules, etc... The script gets separated into individual locations and from then on there is no linear order whatsoever. You may be filming scene #73 on the first day and scene #1 on the last day, with all the other scenes filmed in between with no specific numeric order.

When you shoot a movie with a minuscule budget it is best to try and shoot your scenes in sequence as much as you can. Of course, you should always think about saving money first, but it is a good idea to try and shoot in sequence. It will make it a lot easier for your actors to stay into character and immerse themselves in the story. You will spend less time on the set refreshing their memory as to where they are in the story, and this will save you money because you will be able to shoot more scenes per day. If possible, schedule your scenes to be shot in the same order as the script indicates.

• PRE-PRODUCTION CREW MEETINGS-

Once you have decided on who will be in your cast and crew, it is time to start scheduling crew meetings. Everyone in your crew must attend these meetings. Having an ample amount of crew meetings is a crucial factor in having a crew that works well together. Crew meetings help to keep everyone on the same page throughout the production.

It is generally understood that you do not have to pay people to attend these crew meetings during the pre-production phase. Everyone who works on a low budget movie must understand that their pay begins on the first day of filming, not during pre-production.

Crew meetings should start as soon as you nail down shooting dates with everyone. During the pre-production phase these meetings should be held at your place, or at the place of any of your crew members. They should be about an hour to an hour and a half long. In these meetings, everyone is encouraged to ask questions and offer any information that might benefit your film production. You will lay out your shooting schedule plan as well as all the requirements associated with all the upcoming film shoots.

PRE-PRODUCTION   /   101.

You must lay everything out on the table in these pre-production meetings, both literally, and figuratively. The idea is to give everyone in the meeting a clear idea of what your film vision is and what is expected from them to make it happen.

You should have at least 3 crew meetings during the last week before you start shooting. The first thing you should do is distribute copies of your storyboard and location shot lists, as well as your shooting schedule. Everyone in your crew must get a copy of each item. During these crew meetings you will also discuss the details of your production regarding any technical matters that are involved with the film, such as any lighting set-ups, camera angles, props, etc...

Some of the things you need to discuss with your DP/Cinematographer/Grip during the pre-production meetings are things like what kind of film stock he suggests using for your film, what kind of lighting style he thinks would be good, as well as what style of shooting he plans to use to get things done quickly ("hand-held" camera, "Steadycam", etc..)

You also want to discuss with your Props/Costume person any issues related to props and costumes for each scene. They are in charge of having all of these things at the ready when they are on the set, so make sure you provide them with everything that is needed ahead of time. By the time you have your last pre-production crew meeting your Props/Costume person should have everything they need to do their job when the filming begins.

PRE-PRODUCTION   /   102.

   With your Soundman (person), you want to discuss the placement of microphones for each scene, as well as any other sound related issues. Any location that has a sound issue such as a nearby train track, a noisy freight elevator, a flight path for a nearby airport, etc... should be discussed at these crew meetings.

   As for your AD/Production Manager/Grip; you will want to discuss all the responsibilities they will have on your film shoots in terms of organizing and managing things. They are the one who is in charge of getting everyone on the set, on time, and ready to work. You must stress to them that organization is their key responsibility. In every crew meeting you have throughout your film production it is very important that you make this person aware of everything you will need in terms of cast and crew to film each scene. After that, it is up to them to crack the whip and keep things rolling along smoothly.

   Your Script Supervisor/PA/Grip and the rest of your crew should also receive extensive briefings at your crew meetings regarding all of their duties.

   Once the filming begins, crew meetings should be held regularly at the beginning of each work day. They should last for about 20-30 minutes, and you should discuss in detail with everyone what you will be filming that day and how each person is going to do their job.

Websites that offer software for independent filmmakers to do scheduling, breakdowns, shot lists, etc... :

PRE-PRODUCTION   /   103.

- http://www.junglesoftware.com/index.html

- http://www.blackfishfilms.com/free_software.htm

These programs are very helpful for organizing and planning every aspect of a low budget film production.

- **REHEARSING WITH YOUR ACTORS-**

Besides your crew meetings, you must also have at least 3 rehearsals with your cast during the week before your shooting begins. These should be held separately from your crew meetings. They are two different aspects of your film that require undivided attention on each one.

These meetings should be held much in the same way as your crew meetings, except with rehearsals you are playing more the role of Director instead of the Producer. With rehearsals you must place your attention on the performances and the storyline instead of the technical issues of each scene.

You should start by distributing scripts, storyboards, and shooting schedules to everyone in the cast. Then you want to go over each scene page by page with the actors and tell them anything relevant they might need to know to play their parts. They should be encouraged to take notes and ask questions.

Next, you want to start rehearsing lines with your cast. This should be done at first with scripts in hand. By the time your third rehearsal is finished you should be confident that your cast is ready to film without having scripts in their hands to help them with their lines. If they are not ready, then schedule another rehearsal before filming begins, if you can.

Do not be afraid to demand a lot from your actors. You must show that you are passionate about your story and that you want them to be passionate too. Your goal is to get all of your actors to understand your vision and be ready to interpret it (quickly) when the filming begins the following week.

When you are rehearsing with the cast, make an effort to stress that you will only have 2-3 takes at the most for each shot, then you will have to move on to the next shot. They must understand that your filming ratio is only about 3:1 and you cannot afford to do a lot of takes.

Your Script Supervisor/PA/Grip should attend the last rehearsal. They should watch the actors rehearse and then point out to you any script discrepancies that you might have overlooked.

- **RELEASE FORMS/CONTRACTS-**

EVERYONE YOU HIRE MUST SIGN A RELEASE FORM/CONTRACT. Before anyone begins working for you it is mandatory that you have a release form made up for them and ready to be signed. Every person in your cast and crew must sign one, period. This is basically just a one page document that states the terms of a person's employment. It is your basic short-form contract of employment that will protect your monetary and overall rights to your film.

Certain people that you hire need their own customized release form/contract that explains the deal you have with them (IE; actors must agree to let you use their image and their voice, while cinematographers agree to let you use the images they create on film). In most cases you can use a generic release form template for the people you hire. All you have to do is write up a form that contains general wording about working for you on your film and how you retain all the rights to this work. Leave blank spaces in the parts that describe the details of the job they will be performing and fill them in later when the person is signing the form.

You can make your own forms

While you could hire a lawyer to draw up you release form/contract, you really don't need one. Sure, lawyers have a certain way of presenting legal ease in an impressive manner, but the bottom line is that with a very small film Production you don't have a lot to say in legal terms.
All you need to say is that you are hiring this person to work on your film and that you retain all of the rights to all the products of their efforts.

Your generic release form/contract should look something like this:

RELEASE FORM/ CONTRACT

PRE-PRODUCTION   /   106.

I, _____, agree to hire _____ to work on my film with the title "_____" for their services to be rendered as a(n) _____ on the following dates: _____.

For their services rendered the above mentioned per diem employee will be **compensated as follows**:

They will be **paid** _____ per _____ for _____ days of work for a total of _____ to be paid on_____.

In addition to the monetary compensation described above **they will also receive a film credit** at the end of the film that states their name and job that they performed while working on this film.

A **VHS/DVD copy** of the finished product of the above mentioned film will also be provided to this person as compensation for their work on the film.

_____ retains all the rights to any and all products created by the above mentioned per diem employee while working on the above mentioned film. This includes any images and sound on tape and/or film in any form whether they be un-edited or the finished product.

_____retains all the rights of ownership to the above mentioned film title, including the rights to sell and distribute this film product nationally and worldwide in any format.

PRE-PRODUCTION   /   107.

_____ is not responsible or liable for any injuries that may occur to the above mentioned per diem employee during the filming of the above mentioned film and this per diem employee agrees to work at their own risk.

_____ is not responsible or liable for any damages that may occur to the above mentioned per diem employee's equipment (if provided) during the filming of the above mentioned film.

Signed,

_____ (Per Diem employee's signature)

_____ (Your signature)

_____ Date

   This generic form can be used for your entire cast and crew. You can also use it for any people who do post-production work on your film with such things as sound design or music.

   Make sure you do not forget to state in writing on your release form/contract that YOU RETAIN ALL RIGHTS TO THE FILM. Both you and the employee need to sign and date the bottom, and then you should put the document in a file somewhere at your home. It is the only legal protection you have for your film, so keep a stack of release forms in your briefcase. Make sure you have that briefcase in hand when ever you go to any meeting with any potential per diem (freelance) employee for your film. You should make a habit of getting everyone you hire to sign one right away so you can have a little piece of mind regarding the rights and liabilities you have with your film.

You may not think it is important to protect your rights with such a small movie but believe me, if you have any kind of financial success with your film you will find that the same people who told you "a release form wasn't necessary" suddenly find it necessary to hire a lawyer and sue you for a lot of money.

You can type up your own release forms on your home computer or go to a copy and publishing place like *Kinko's* where they will do it for a reasonable price.

• PROPS AND COSTUMES-

As I stated in previous sections, you should keep the costumes and props to a minimum on a low budget film. The strength of your movie depends on your storyline and your actor's abilities, not special effects or fancy clothing.

I have always designed and made all of the props and costumes for my movies. In order to do this one must be very resourceful, and creative. You need to look at ordinary items and find a way to make them extraordinary. For instance, I once used an old copper tea server as a "magic lamp" for a scene that involved a genie. Another time I wrapped a large, black, silk scarf around my head and put a large, plastic ruby on the front to make the costume of a fortune teller.

There are several ways to get props and costumes for your movie: buy them, pay someone to make them, or make them yourself. The last way is the best way to do it if you really want to save a lot of money. Hiring people to make costumes and props is very expensive, so I suggest that you find a way to do it yourself.

The truth of the matter is you can find just about anything you need to make all the props and costumes in your movie without spending a lot of your budget money.

Garage sales and flea markets can be a goldmine

The best way that I have found to locate props and costumes is at garage sales and flea markets. All of the stuff that is being sold are things that the owners do not want anymore, so you can usually buy them for pennies. People sell just about anything at these places, and sometimes their trash is your treasure. That old wooden box that some person thought was worthless could make a great treasure box for a flashback scene that involves pirates. That blue and white striped turtleneck shirt from the sixties that someone is selling for 10 cents would be perfect for a character that is supposed to be in the Russian navy. You can find furniture, dolls, books, silverware, fake weapons, jewelry, clothing, shoes, boots, and just about anything else you want at these places. You can even find complete costumes sometimes for just pennies at a garage sale or a flea market. A lot of people keep the Halloween costumes that they have made or bought over the years. They usually discover these items buried in a closet when they clean out their house or move to another one. A lot of these costumes can be very authentic looking, and may have cost a lot of money to buy or taken many hours to make, and yet there they are selling for pennies at a garage sale! While the original owners may have no more use for them, these costumes can be a goldmine for an independent filmmaker.

I have found many costumes over the years at garage sales. One time I bought a complete Russian Cossack dancer outfit for fifty cents. The person I bought it from made the whole outfit by hand. It was very impressive looking, right down to the matching fur hat and boots. They had used it only once when they were younger for a dance routine they performed in college. This costume took on a whole new life when I featured it in a flashback *period* scene in one of my first movies.

Any suburb will do just fine

To find a garage sale or flea market all you have to do is drive around any suburban neighborhood on a weekend and look for the garage sale signs posted on telephone poles, trees and street signs. These cardboard signs will have the address and directions on it. There is usually a series of signs with arrows along the route that points the way.
The best time to go is early on Saturday morning. This is when you will find the best selection of stuff at garage sales or flea markets. There are also garage sales on Fridays and Sundays too, but the best ones are on Saturday. You can also look in the classified sections of any local newspaper for garage sale and flea market advertisements.

Have fun with the process

Finding a garage sale or flea market is like going on a treasure hunt. You are following clues to places you have never been before to find a variety of items at very good prices. While it is actually work that you are doing for your film production, somehow it just doesn't seem like work. It is more like a scavenger hunt than it is work. It can be a lot of fun.

Bring your script breakdown

You should always have your script breakdown with you whenever you go on the search for props, costumes, etc... This will be your list of things you need to find on your scavenger hunt.

It is a good idea to look for the most important things on your lists first. You can get them out of the way and there will not be as much pressure on you to find them as your deadline to begin filming approaches.

Drive a hard bargain

Do not be afraid to negotiate for deals. If a person at a garage sale or flea market asks you how much you are willing to pay for an item you should always give a really low offer. Remember, the item this person is trying to sell to you is something that they no longer want, so it can't be worth that much to them. Give offers in cents, not dollars. You will be surprised at what you can buy at a garage sale for a nickel if you are bold enough to offer. A lot of the time the people are just going through the motions when they ask a price. They really just want to get rid of their junk; they are not looking to get rich.

If you really *need* a specific costume of a period or time in history and you do not think that you can put it together yourself, and you cannot find one a garage sale then the best thing to do is rent one from any costume/party shop. Just look in any yellow pages under "costumes" to find a costume shop in any city near your house. You may be able to negotiate a deal on the price for the rental of your costume if you offer the owner of the shop a "special thanks" film credit with their name at the end of your film.

Once you have all your props and costumes, you must store them in clear, plastic containers, and label each one with detailed information. When you are ready to film you will be giving these items to your Props/Costume/Grip person. It will be their responsibility to provide these items to you on the set when needed. They will be in charge of these items while you are actually filming, but you are in charge of them the rest of the time. These items will stay in your house before and after film shoots, and when you are on the road filming they will be kept in your car/truck/van.

• BUYING FILM-

If you want to make a movie with a very, very low budget, you have to shoot it on 16mm film. While almost every major movie you see in the theaters is shot on 35mm film, most of the smaller films that screen at film festivals are shot on 16mm. This is because you can get almost the same quality image on the movie screen for about 1/3 of the cost of 35mm. 16mm allows small films to be" in The Game" without having to pay like the "Big Boys".

From the actual cost of the film stock, to the cost of making a final print, everything is much more expensive with 35mm. I strongly suggest that you shoot your movie on 16mm film for it is much more affordable than 35mm and the image quality is comparable. If your movie happens to get picked up by a major distributor for theaters then you can always have your film blown-up to a 35mm print later on.

Kodak is King

For me, there is only one kind of film that you should use to shoot a movie and that is **KODAK film**. I have tried film from other companies like Fuji, but I found that their image quality was inferior to Kodak's. For example, I felt that the colors of the Fuji film were just too soft for my standards. No other film has the sharpness and color quality of Kodak film.

Consult with your DP/Cinematographer/Grip

Before you buy your Kodak film to shoot your movie, you must decide on what particular film stock you want to use (Kodak Vision 7229, 7246, 7277, etc...). This is a very important decision for it is a big factor in determining the "look" of your film. You must consult with your DP/Cinematographer about what film stock you should use. Tell them the kind of *look* you want for your film, and they will tell you what particular film stock you will need to achieve that *look*. The kind of things you should discuss to

PRE-PRODUCTION   /   114.

determine the *look* of your film are things like the mood of the film (uplifting, depressing, happy, etc...), the period (old west, futuristic, dark ages, etc...), and the locations (Interior, Exterior, bright sunlight, low light, etc...).

After you have decided on the type of film to use, you must figure out how much film stock to buy. This will be determined by your DP/Cinematographer/Grip. Both of you must go through your script scene by scene and approximate how many feet of film it will take to shoot each one using a 3:1 filming ratio (how many takes you will shoot of each shot to get the one you will use). Then, add up all up the footage needed for each scene and you will have the total amount of film stock footage that you will need to shoot your film.

There are many different places to buy Kodak film, but I suggest you go straight to Kodak. Sure, some places advertise Kodak film for a cheaper price than Kodak sells it for, but I suggest you steer clear of them. It may be the same product Kodak sells but you have no way of knowing if the film was damaged in the shipping or storing process. Kodak is very, very, careful to protect their film stock during every aspect of it's film life at their facilities. It is stored, handled, and delivered with the utmost care. Places that buy Kodak film wholesale and sell it at a bargain price may not be so diligent in taking care of the film they sell.

Even when it is sealed in it's protective canister film is very sensitive to heat and light conditions. It can be damaged or even ruined if absolute care has not been taken during every aspect of it's film life. Yes, you could buy film at a bargain outlet and save some money. However, if that film happened to be left in the back of a hot delivery truck with the sun beating down on it for hours then there is a good chance that you have bought damaged film and you would not even know it until it is developed. In other words; all of your money and effort you spend to shoot your film will all be for nothing.

Do not buy from anyone "short ends" or film that is left over from various other film shoots. A lot of places sell pieces of film at a very good price. This sounds like a good deal, but in this case; buyer beware. You do not know where that film has been or how it was handled once the can was cracked open.

Film stock and the related costs is the one aspect of your film production where you cannot afford to be cheap. Film is far too delicate to trust in the hands of anyone who does not have the best reputation in the industry for this product.

Do not jeopardize your whole film project by purchasing your 16mm film at any place other than Kodak's official sales locations. If there is not a Kodak facility in the city nearest to where you live, then you can purchase your film from them over the phone and have it delivered to your house.

Below is the toll free phone number you can call to order Kodak film over the phone:

Eastman Kodak- 1(800) 621-3456

PRE-PRODUCTION   /   116.

Below is a link to a web page on Kodak.com that offers information about all the different types of 16mm film stock they sell:

•http://www.kodak.com/US/en/motion/16mm/products/negative/?id=0.1.4.5.4&lc=en

   Once you have received your 16mm Kodak film, be sure to store it in a cool, dark, dry place until you are ready to start shooting.

   • **MAKING TRAVEL ARRANGEMENTS-**

   Providing your cast and crew with a hotel room and food for a day is expensive, so you should try to limit your travel time to one week. If you can do it in five days, that is even better. The desire to drive to a wilderness location and shoot at a more relaxed pace without interference from other people must be tempered with the idea that less days on the road is better. The whole idea is to go and film your scenes in as few days as possible and return home promptly.

   Before you go on a road trip with your cast and crew you must do a lot of work preparing ahead of time. Making the proper travel arrangements is the key to having a successful road trip film shoot. You must be sure that you make the experience as painless as possible for your cast and crew so they will stay motivated and focused on your film project. If things go awry for them in terms of accommodations, food, or traveling situation, they will start complaining, and that is when they might decide to just forget you and your little movie. They could desert you if things get too bad, and needless to say this would be a disaster. Keep your traveling situation on track, and your film production will stay on track. If you do not prepare adequately for your road trip film shoots then you will run into a lot of problems that will cost you time and money.

Provide Maps and Directions for everyone

One of the most important things to do is make sure you provide everyone in your caravan with detailed maps and directions that describes exactly how to get to your destination. It is your responsibility to do all of the research on how to get to any locations, as well as the printing work.

Websites that give maps, driving directions, community information, population, etc... :

- http://www.mapquest.com/

- http://www.uslocalmap.com/

- http://www.mapnation.com/

- http://www.randmcnally.com/

Once you have done all the research for maps and driving directions, then you must make copies and distribute them to everyone right before you get on the road.

A Laptop (or Notebook) computer is a valuable item to have on a low budget film shoot.

It is a good idea to bring a laptop (or notebook) computer that has wireless internet capability when you go out on a location shoot. You should also bring a portable printer. There are many benefits that come with having a notebook computer on a film shoot. One of those benefits is being able to make your hotel/motel reservations when you are on the road. A good time to perform this task is when you stop to fill up for gas. You can even do it while you are on the highway, as long as you are not the driver. A laptop/notebook computer is also a great item to have on location to do such things as production notes, shooting schedules, release forms and travel arrangements. It is also great for making changes to the script. Another great benefit is being able to access information on the internet that is related to your story. Let's say you wanted to add something to your script that has to do with an event that happened in ancient history: you can research the topic on the internet while you are on location to make sure that you are historically accurate.

Watch the weather

Monitoring the weather forecasts for the areas you will be traveling through on your way to your destination is very important. You must be aware of any possible bad weather that may affect your driving time. You must also be sure that everyone in the caravan is prepared for the conditions they may encounter on the road. For example; if you are going to a mountain area in the winter time and there is any chance of snow, then you better make sure that every car in your caravan has a set of tire chains on board.

PRE-PRODUCTION   /   119.

It is a good idea to watch *The Weather Channel* on television up to the moment you leave, as well as every night in your hotel room when you are on the road. If you want more in-depth weather research than the television version offers then you can go on the internet and peruse their website. There are also a number of other websites that will tell you everything about the weather for anywhere you may travel. You can use your notebook computer to visit these websites any time you need a weather update when you are filming out on location. If you do not have wireless internet capability, then try to stay at a motel/hotel that offers free internet access with your stay. You should ask at the time you are making your reservations if this amenity is offered at any potential motel/hotel.

Websites that give weather forecasts and weather related information:

- http://www.uslocalweather.com/

- http://www.noaa.gov/wx.html

- http://wwwa.accuweather.com/

- http://www.weather.com/index.html

Must have a cell phone

It is mandatory that you bring a cell phone with you on your road trip film shoots. This is especially important if you do not have a laptop/notebook computer with wireless internet capability.

PRE-PRODUCTION   /   120.

   A cell phone can be used for such things as calling in food orders, taking digital stills of your scenes, accessing the internet, making hotel reservations, and keeping in touch with your caravan members while you are in transit. Your cell phone is your main communication and electronic utility device when you are on the road. Every car in your caravan must have at least one person in it that has a cell phone. The last thing you want is to lose someone on the road and not be able to communicate with them. This will cost you valuable time searching for the lost party that could have been used to drive towards your destination. The sooner you get there, film your movie, and come home, the sooner you can stop paying everyone that is involved with it. Your cell phone is a valuable device that keeps you in touch with everyone. It also helps to keep you moving forward, which will help save you time and money in the long run.

Stay near a *cell*

   Keep in mind that a cell phone is not a satellite phone. You cannot go to all corners of the earth and expect to get reception. You must be within the broadcast zone of the nearest *cell* (transmitter*)* that is owned or used by the company you signed up with for your cell phone plan. This is one of the reasons it is a good idea to stay near a semi-large town when you go out into the wilderness to shoot your film. This way you can be guaranteed that your cell phone and/or your notebook computer with wireless internet capability will get reception. Having a good-sized town nearby is also helpful in the event that you need something from a store, or if someone happens to get injured.

PRE-PRODUCTION   /   121.

   The ideal situation for a person who is making a movie with a very, very low budget would be no road trip at all. Instead of shooting at some far away locations, you shoot your whole movie at locations in and around the area where you and everyone working on your production happens to live. This way you could save the $5000 that you would have spent on travel arrangements, and use it for post-production costs instead. If you can manage to do that, then great, but if you must take your cast and crew on the road to film any part of your movie, then this is how you should do it:

1. Always wait until the day you are ready to leave before you make your motel/hotel reservations for everyone in your cast and crew.

   Plan your lodging situation wisely. You may think you have people nailed down as a confirmation to work, but they can cancel at the last minute, and cost you money. Most motels/hotels require at least a twenty-four hour cancellation notice ahead of time once you have made your reservations. If you cancel at the last minute they will charge the price of the room on the credit card you gave them over the phone or online when you made the reservations.

Beware of cancellations

   It is a daunting task to get everyone together on a road trip for a location shoot on a low budget film. There are many reasons why this is true, but the fact is; you may have some last minute cancellations. If this happens, do not panic. Unless it is one of your principal actors, your

DP/Cinematographer/Grip, your Soundman (person)/Grip, or your Assistant Director/Production Manager/Grip, you should not cancel your trip. Not to minimize the efforts of the other people in your cast and crew, but the aforementioned group of people are the only ones that you just cannot do without on your location film shoot.

If you have a last minute cancellation by someone who is not one of the most important people in your film production, then you and everyone else in the crew will just have to pick up the extra slack that this person will create (in terms of work load). For example; if your Boom Operator/Audio Assistant/Grip cancels at the last minute, then choose one or more of your employees that do not have a heavy work load and have them do that job when they are not doing the job you originally hired them to do. You can do this job yourself (which I have done many times on many of my film shoots) or you can use some of your actor "extras" to do it. You can even use someone like your Script Supervisor/PA/Grip to help with this job. They may not have experience holding a boom microphone on a film shoot, but they can learn how to do it very quickly. That particular job is not that hard to learn. It is more physical than mental. The Soundman (person) who brought the DAT recorder package is the one that you are paying to *think* when you are recording the sound for your movie, not their assistant. They are pretty much just taking directions from you and the Soundman (person).

If you are forced to reassign a job at the last minute; just write the new stipulation into the release form of whomever you reassign the job to and add a little extra pay to their payment plan. Make sure you have them sign a copy of it before you leave town and file that copy away somewhere safe.

Cancel a film shoot only if absolutely necessary

When you are faced with the decision of whether or not to cancel a road trip film shoot you must take into consideration the level of importance of the people who canceled on you. If someone major like the star of your film or the DP/Cinematographer/Grip cancels on you, then the whole film shoot must be rescheduled. You cannot film without either one of those people. Canceling a road trip film shoot at the last minute should be done only as a last resort. You could lose all the money for all of the rooms you secured with your credit card. When you consider that means you, your cast, and your entire crew, it can be a lot of money wasted from your meager budget.

I strongly suggest that you wait until you are driving in your cars with your cast and crew in a caravan on the freeway before you make your final motel/hotel reservations with your cell phone. Of course, that does not mean that you travel to your certain area without doing research on the motel/hotels beforehand. It just means that you should wait until everyone is accounted for and in transit with you on your road trip before you make that call on your cell phone that locks you in for the night on all the rooms to accommodate everyone involved with your location film shoot.

Travel related websites that are very helpful for doing research on any hotels/motels (or

other travel related issues) for almost any area you might plan to travel to for location film shoots:

- http://www.travelocity.com/

- http://www.priceline.com/

- http://www.expedia.com/

Before you leave you should research the motels/hotels in the area that you plan to film near, and then write down in a small notepad the entire list of phone numbers and website addresses of the places with the best deals (or *save* the info in your notebook computer). If one place fills up, then you still have your list of other motel/hotels to choose from that you can refer to when you are driving on the road and making your room reservations for the night using your laptop or your cell phone.

2. Bring/buy a lot of food that is easy to eat on the fly.

Most of the meals you provide should be things like sandwiches, burritos, or veggie wraps. These are things that can be made by you the night before a film shoot, or purchased in bulk at a warehouse type store. You can also order a lot of these type of meals "to go" at restaurants on the road. The kind of meals that I am talking about are things that are *easy* to eat and don't cause too much of a mess when you are eating them in the car. You want to try and avoid any sit down meals at restaurants with your entire cast and crew. This will only take time out of your busy schedule, and cost you money in service tips.

Warehouse stores are great for low budget film shoots

It is a good idea to visit a warehouse type grocery store like *Costco,* or *Sam's Club* before you leave on a film shoot road trip. These places sell a variety of food that is good to bring on these trips. You can buy pre-made, easy to eat meals in bulk, and the prices are very good for your small budget. You can also buy a variety of beverages like sodas, bottled waters, and fruit juices. It is a lot cheaper to do it this way than it is to buy everyone beverages at mini-marts on the road. You can also buy a couple of large ice chests at one of these warehouse stores; one to keep your perishables fresh, and one to keep your beverages cold. You can get your daily ice for these ice chests at the motel/hotels that you are staying at, and this will also save you a little money out of your road trip budget.

3. Bring a lot of ready-to-eat snacks that are quick and easy to consume.

Whether you are on a long drive with no restaurants in sight, or a long film shoot that forces you to postpone lunch for a while, quick and easy snacks can prevent major backlash from the effects of your cast and crew not having eaten in a while. Sometimes low budget film shoots must require everyone to endure brutally long working and traveling hours. The last thing you want to do is make your cast and crew too hungry to work, or travel, so you must always have some sort of temporary fix to the problem of not being able to eat a legitimate meal. Beef jerky, granola bars, chips, candy bars, nuts, fruit, and cookies are all good things to keep on hand. You can also buy these items in bulk at *Costco* or *Sam's Club* for a good price.

4. Be smart with hotel reservations

If you plan to travel in the morning to a far away location and then film during the second half of the day, be sure that you make your room reservations before you leave or before you begin the day of filming. One time I failed to do this and it cost me dearly. I made the mistake of just blowing through town with my caravan and heading straight out to the film location without making reservations. I saw that the motel was empty and figured we would be fine. That was a bad decision. Don't assume that the motels in the nearby town will have plenty of rooms available when you finish shooting just because they looked empty when you passed through town earlier in the day. One busload of people, a caravan of travelers, or a special event in town that you did not know about can fill up the rooms of a small town in a blink of the eye.

If you cannot find rooms at the end of the day then your shoot for the next day could be ruined. In a worst case scenario; your whole cast and crew will desert you because of your irresponsible behavior. You must be a responsible coordinator among many other things when you make your own movie. You must portray a figure of authority and confidence throughout your production, or nobody will follow you anywhere. You are in charge of your film and you must always show this through your behavior.

I experienced the nightmare of not being able to find any rooms available once before when I was shooting in the

PRE-PRODUCTION   /   127.

Sierra Mountains near Bishop, California. The town was deserted when I blew through early in the morning, so I did not bother to make motel reservations. After a long day of filming nearby, I returned to town only to find it packed with people who had flooded into town all day long to attend the annual "Mule Days" event (some sort of Rodeo) that was scheduled to begin in a couple of days. Not one room was available, and I had to drive halfway back to Los Angeles to find a room. Some of my cast and crew deserted me. They made the long drive home to Los Angeles on a desert highway through the Owens Valley in the middle of the night after an exhausting day of filming. Needless to say, it was a disaster for them and for me as well. I had to do some creative script changes, and hire a new cast and crew.

I lost a lot of money on that day, but it will never happen to me again. "Live and learn", as the saying goes.

I will never again assume that there will always be rooms available at the local motels/hotels after I am done filming. ALWAYS MAKE YOUR MOTEL/HOTEL RESERVATIONS BEFORE STARTING YOUR DAY OF FILMING.

When you are organizing a location shoot with very limited funds to grease the wheels of production it is sometimes hard to confirm everyone will show up until the day before. Whether it is a lack of respect because of lacking funds, or just a matter of waiting to the last minute to see if something else better to work on might come up, people tend to leave their options open with you until the last minute. This is why you should not make your motel reservations weeks before the shoot. Make your motel/hotel reservations the day before you leave, or even the same day you leave. Do not make them any further ahead, for things could change (people get sick and cancel, unexpected weather problems, etc...) and you will lose your deposit on any rooms you cancel on. You may even end up paying the full price for every room.

Travel research helps to avoid problems

The best way to avoid problems with getting motel/hotel rooms is to do research on the local motels and the town near your potential location. This research can be done when you go out to do a location scout. Stop in at each motel and get a business card or a brochure with room rates. While you are there, ask the person at the front desk if there are any special events scheduled to happen in their town in the near future.

Schedule your film shoots during times when there are NO SPECIAL EVENTS in that town. This will eliminate one factor that could leave you stranded without a room. Your motel room is a staging point for everything while you are shooting on location, and the rooms of small town motels fill up quickly, so don't take them for granted.

You will also save money by avoiding lodging in a small town during times of special events, for room rates and everything else in town are usually more expensive during these times.

Find out what the slowest time of the year is for any town that you plan to lodge at near a location, and schedule your film shoots during that time (off season). There will be less people, and everything (including room rates) will be less expensive. All of this research should be done when you go to scout locations. This research will help your location shoots go more smoothly, and save you money.

5. Always be in command of your plan

Indecisiveness, ineptness, or irresponsible behavior must not be displayed by you in any way when you are in charge of a film production. You are the leader of your project and you must act like a leader. You will have many responsibilities to juggle during the process of your film production but there is one very important responsibility that should always be at the top of your list of things to do; you must take care of everyone's basic needs in your cast and crew. If you do not, they will lose faith in you, and desert you for sure. For example; not being able to provide a motel room for them at the end of a long day of filming is unforgivable in their eyes. It shows that you did not plan very well. Remember, these people are employees, not friends, and they will leave you if you slip up once too often.

When you are doing the pre-production work on your film it is important that you understand that putting forth a great deal of effort during this phase means that you will have less problems during the production phase. You want to make sure that everything is ready for filming before you begin shooting. The idea here is to prevent costly delays in your production schedule because of unforeseen problems. Do your pre-production homework, and things will go smoothly during the big test (filming).

7

Production

By the time you finish up with your extensive preparation process you will be anxious to get the camera rolling. You should be absolutely ready to go before you begin filming. What this means is; when there are no foreseeable problems left unresolved. DO NOT START FILMING UNTIL YOU ARE COMPLETELY READY. If you do, you will waste time and money with the down-time you spend fixing problems, while everybody and everything you are paying for at that time gets to sit around and get paid for nothing.

While the pre-production aspect of a film can be tedious at times, the actual filming tends to be the *fun* part (as long as everything is going right). It is the time when your film vision becomes reality. If you have a little talent, a lot of motivation, and a good crew, your film vision becomes *art*.

There is nothing more fulfilling for a filmmaker than a good day of filming. Watching a cast and crew bring your story to life on film is a wonderful feeling. It makes all the hard work very much worth the effort.

Filming gives me somewhat of a liberating and euphoric feeling. Before I make a movie, for many months, or possibly even years I dream of the moment my vision will become a reality. Every aspect of my film project dominates my thought process during the period before filming begins. I have one goal in mind: get this film "in the can"! When I finally get to see it happen, it feels like a burden has been lifted from my shoulders. Although I know that I will still have a lot of work left to do in the post-production phase to complete my vision, getting the film "in the can" always feels like a major victory to me. If making a movie is like running in a marathon race, then the filming part is definitely the endorphin high.

• PRODUCTION CAST AND CREW MEETINGS-

As I stated in the section about pre-production, having cast and crew meetings on a regular basis is essential to your success with a low budget film production. Once you start the filming process these meetings should take place at the beginning of each film shoot. You should hold these meetings on the location or set where you will be filming that day. If it is a location that you do not have the luxury to hang around at then you should hold your meetings in a nearby public location; any place such as a park or rest area will do just fine.

Although your cast and crew meetings will be held at the same place when you are on a film shoot, they should be held at separate times. As I stated earlier; these are two completely different aspects of your film that need your undivided attention, one at a time.

- **TIPS FOR A SUCCESSFUL LOW BUDGET FILM PRODUCTION**

Be resourceful, and be active

For example; if you are filming a scene outside in the desert and there are scattered clouds in the sky, you should discuss a contingency plan for filming that day in case it starts to rain. Do not let a whole day go by without filming something just because of bad weather. You still have to pay your cast, crew, and equipment rental place for that day, bad weather or not. If there is something that you can film in a nearby town under a public awning or even back in your hotel room, then do it. Be resourceful and film something involving rain that can replace the part you were planning to film before the rain began to fall. Use the rain.

You should never have *down time* once you begin filming

You must never be idle on a low budget film shoot. You have to keep the film production ball rolling no matter what happens. Crew meetings are essential to the process of keeping the ball rolling because you can discuss potential problems and make plans to deal with them quickly should they arise.

Protect your film equipment at all times

You also want to discuss a plan to keep the film equipment and film stock dry if it suddenly starts to rain. You do not want to be out in the middle of the desert (or anywhere) with your film equipment and film stock unprotected when the rain begins to fall. You should always have a few umbrellas and a couple of plastic tarps with you at all times when you are filming outside to protect your equipment from the rain until you can get all of it quickly moved inside a nearby automobile. If you cannot keep a van or a car nearby for quick shelter from the rain, then make sure you have some other sort of cover like a cave, or a canopy. Film and film equipment do not go well with water. The smallest amount of water can ruin a camera, a microphone, or a roll of film, so you should always have an overprotective plan to keep them dry.

Dirt, sand and dust are also enemies of film equipment. These items can cause scratches in your film negative and cause major damage to the intricate workings of expensive cameras, lenses, and recorders. Proper protection from these elements should also be in place for your equipment when you are filming in areas where these elements are abundant, such as the desert, an abandoned house, etc... This should be discussed during crew meetings with your DP/Cinematographer/Grip, your Soundman (person), and anyone else who will be using film equipment throughout the day of filming.

Keep your cast informed

As for your cast meetings; the most important things to discuss should be any difficult or demanding parts that will be filmed that day/night, such as emotional scenes or complex action scenes. You should also talk about the rundown (order) of scenes that will be shot that day/night, and how long you will be shooting. By discussing these types of things ahead of time you give the actors time to prepare for the stuff that will be expected from them.

If you are filming in a public place with a lot of people around you do not want to stop down in the middle of a shoot to give an actor his "motivation" for a particular line or to tell them the blocking for their entry and exit of a scene. Make sure they know what is expected from them well ahead of time. Most of these type of questions were already answered in the pre-production rehearsals, but sometimes people forget them by the time filming begins, so be ready to explain them again in cast and crew meetings during the production phase.

The things that you should discuss at production cast and crew meetings are as follows:

1. The shot list for that day.

2. Important productions details.

3. How long you expect the work day/night to last.

4. A contingency plan for filming in the event of bad weather.

5. How to protect film equipment from the elements.

6. Safety instructions.

7. Any foreseeable difficulties that may be presented during the day/night of filming ahead.

The AD/Production Manager/Grip and the Script Supervisor/PA/Grip both play a big part in your cast and crew meetings. It is the job of the AD/Production Manager/Grip to gather everyone together to hold these meetings. This person will also mediate the proceedings of the crew meetings, while the cast meetings will be mediated by the Script Supervisor/PA/Grip.

The AD/Production Manager/Grip needs to know ahead of time about any questions or problems the cast and crew may have that are related to the production process so they can present them to you during these meetings. Throughout your filming process your AD/Production Manager/Grip works closely with everyone in your cast and crew, so they usually know all about any production-related issues that are going on without having to ask too many questions.

Stick to the Script

The Script/Supervisor/PA/Grip is in charge of discussing any dialogue or script related problems that any actors may have, as well as any production issues that might compromise the story. While you should be open to any creative interpretations that any actor might offer that might be different from the way that you envisioned it in your head, do not allow any changes in your dialogue. Your words tell *your* story. You are banking on the storyline of your movie to make it a success; if you start changing the dialogue of every scene to please all your actors then you will have a completely different story by the time you are done filming. Maybe it will be a better story, but most likely it will not. Instead you will have a jumbled mess of several different stories slapped together to form one great big, terrible story. Since you are the one who is (most likely) putting up the money for your film you cannot take any chances that would lead to this unfortunate event. Stick to your script and you will avoid this problem.

Bring a briefcase full of scripts

The Script Supervisor/PA/Grip is in charge of having all the script copies that are needed on the set and at any production-related meetings. They need to carry a briefcase full of copies of your script with them at all times when they are working on your movie. When you are in the act of filming this person needs to have a copy of your script in their hands that is open on the scene that it being filmed. They need to follow along with the actors as they read their lines and write down notes on the script that describes any dialogue or storyline violations. Their main concern is *continuity*. If there are any ad-lib lines added by any actors while you are filming, it is their job to decide if the lines will work with your storyline. If they do not work, then they must tell you right away. If someone is not reading their lines properly (as written) then the Script Supervisor/PA/Grip needs to tell you right away.

At the end of each take the Script Supervisor/PA/Grip needs to bring to your attention any major violations that just occurred. They should not bother you with minor violations until there is a break in the filming. If there is a major violation they need to tell you immediately so you can yell "Cut!" right away. The sooner you yell "Cut" and stop the filming of that particular take, the less film you waste on a shot that has been deemed "unusable" by the

Script Supervisor/PA/Grip. Remember, this person was hired by you to know your script better than you know it yourself, so if they decided it does not meet your standards, and it was necessary to tell you in the middle of a take, then it is usually a serious enough script or storyline violation to warrant stopping down the camera.

Script Supervisor/PA/Grip must pay attention

Your Script Supervisor/PA/Grip is also in charge of feeding your actors dialogue when they forget their lines. In a perfect world none of your actors would forget any of their lines in any of the scenes you film. Unfortunately, we live in the real world. No matter how much rehearsing you do with your actors, most of them will forget some of their lines. Some actors are better than others at memorizing lines, but none are one hundred percent fool-proof.

The Script Supervisor/PA/Grip must watch every actor closely when the camera is rolling. When it becomes apparent to them that someone has forgotten their lines as the camera is rolling they have to immediately take action and feed the actor their lines. They must be on the ball and ready to quickly yell out the first few words of the lines that the actor is having trouble with and hopefully this effort will jar the actor's memory. If it is done properly the actor should be able to quickly recover and continue on with the correct dialogue without having to stop down the camera. You can edit out the part where the Script Supervisor/PA/Grip yelled out the actor's lines. If they recover but still don't "nail it", you can re-do the dialogue on the next take. You can also use footage from a previous take to cover those particular lines. The last thing you want to do is shut down in the middle of any take and do it over again, unless you absolutely have to. If the actor does not pick up the dialogue (right away), then it is time for you to yell "Cut!", but only as a last resort.

Rehearse before filming

As for rehearsals, if you are not required to get in and out of a location fast, then you should have a quick rehearsal on the set before the filming of every scene. If you are shooting in a public location and you do not have the luxury of being relaxed on the set, then rehearse at a nearby park or rest area before you go in and shoot the scene. Remember, your actors must know their lines *well* before you shoot any scenes. If they do not know their lines well, it will cost you money in wasted film and time (time is money). You should rehearse with your actors during the pre-production phase until you are confident that all of them will be able to film every scene without a script in their hands. If they are *not* ready, then keep rehearsing until they *are* ready. As I said earlier, you do not have to pay people for pre-production meetings or rehearsals. You only have to pay people for the days that you are actually filming, so make sure you do all of your planning and rehearsing during the pre-production phase.

People should be encouraged to ask questions and voice their opinions at all cast and crew meetings. Everyone involved should speak up about anything that concerns the welfare of the film shoot.

Everyone must multi-task

One of the main things that you must stress at every cast and crew meeting is that no-one is an island in terms of their job. Every person has to do several jobs when you are filming, and no-one is allowed to complain about it. Everyone must help out in every way they can in order to get your film made as smoothly and as quickly as possible. Whether it is carrying equipment, holding a light reflector, or cleaning up after a meal, everyone is expected to do their fair share of the work.

- **SAFETY-**

Safety should be your paramount concern on any film shoot. Even though your film outfit should work fast, that does not mean that you should be reckless. You must be careful that there are no accidents and that no-one gets hurt. If someone gets seriously injured (or worse) while working on one of your film shoots, it is safe to say that your film dream will suddenly turn into a nightmare. Everyone agreed to work at their own risk when they signed their release forms, but it is still *your* job to remind them about safety throughout the production. SAFETY SHOULD BE YOUR NUMBER ONE CONCERN when you are filming. It should be discussed at every cast and crew meeting.

Everyone in your outfit must understand that no film is worth getting seriously hurt or killed over. Often people will feel a sense of liberation when they are working on a low budget film. This can lead to a willingness to take risks in the name of creativity. Your DP/Cinematographer/Grip might be tempted to get a really awesome shot from on top of a building, or one of your actors might want to get closer to the edge of a cliff to make an action scene seem more realistic, but it is not worth the risk. If someone falls from the roof of a building or off a cliff, your film career will be over, there may be legal implications, and if you have a conscience, you will be racked with guilt for the rest of your life.

Bring Fire Extinguishers

Whether you are filming in an old abandoned building in a downtown area or out in the wide open desert, it is always a good idea to have at least two fire extinguishers with you at all times. Even if you are not using any fire in your scenes it is still a good idea to bring them. Things can happen; fires can start anywhere at any time when you are filming. Somebody could drop a cigarette butt on the ground that is still burning, or someone's car could have a wiring problem that causes it to ignite. There is always a possibility of a fire getting started accidentally. You could have a major problem on your hands if you do not bring any fire extinguishers; a fire could start up and the only thing you will have to put it out will be the small bottle of *Evian* water that you are holding in your hand. Make sure the fire extinguishers you bring are brand new or recently re-filled, or they might not work when you need them.

Bring a good first aid kit

A really good first aid kit is mandatory. I am not talking about one of those little boxes that could fit in your pocket, I am talking about one that is at least the size of a shoe box and has a variety of objects inside that includes things like rubbing alcohol, bandages, tape, aspirin, ibuprofen, sun screens, bug repellent, tourniquets, splints, instant ice-packs, etc... You must keep your first aid kit with you on the set at all times. It would be very irresponsible of you to not have one.

Know the way to the hospital

It is also mandatory to know where the nearest hospital is located whenever you are filming out on location. You must do research ahead of time (during the pre-production phase) and keep this information with you at all times when you are filming. You cannot wait for help to arrive if someone gets seriously hurt. There is no time to wait for paramedics in an emergency situation because they might be many miles away. Of course, that is assuming that your cell phone had reception in your remote area and you were able to call 911. If there is a medical emergency during one of your film shoots, you must make the urgent drive to the hospital yourself with your own vehicle. You can call 911 while you are driving towards the nearest town so that a dispatcher can call the emergency room and tell them that you are on your way. You hope that you never have to make that trip, but you have to know the route just in case. You can get information about the hospitals in a particular area at any of the websites for maps and directions that I have provided on previous pages (links).

Bring a lot of water

It is a good idea to bring several gallons of extra water whenever you go on a location film shoot (in addition to your drinking water). These gallons can be used for such things as refilling a radiator if someone's car overheats, washing something out of somebody's eye, or for washing dirty stuff that needs cleaning when you are out in the middle of no-where (dirty costumes, dirty hands, props, etc...) It is also a good idea to bring a large bucket for washing these things and plenty of towels for drying them.

AAA is a *Plus*

I strongly suggest that you join the Auto Club (AAA) and keep your card in your wallet at all times when you are on a road trip film shoot. If you have been a member for at least a year then you have the option to upgrade your membership to AAA *Plus*. You can use your card to get discounts at hotels/motels, retail stores, restaurants, etc… It can also save you a lot of money in towing costs if your car breaks down. You get 2 free tows per year that includes 110 free towing miles for each tow with the AAA *Plus* membership. With the standard membership you only get 7 free miles and then you have to pay for anything that goes over that amount.

It costs approximately $90-120 annually for the AAA *Plus* membership (depending on whether you include your spouse, family, etc...) but it is well worth the money when you consider that you could spend several hundred dollars, or even thousands in towing fees if you break down in a remote area.

We have all seen the television commercials that show the tow truck drivers grinning from ear-to-ear as they hook up some poor sap's broken down car to their tow truck on a desert highway. We all know why those grungy-looking tow truck drivers are always smiling ($$$). Your AAA *Plus* card can protect you from guys like that who charge exorbitant prices to tow your car to the nearest town. I am not saying that you won't have to deal with guys like that if your car breaks down in the middle of nowhere, I am only saying that if you are a AAA *Plus* member, you won't have to pay for the towing. 110 miles of free towing should be plenty enough to get you to the nearest town where you can get your car fixed, and get back on the road.

   AAA is the original roadside service and travel club in America and they really take care of their members. Almost every town in the United States has a tow truck driver that will honor your AAA card. No matter where it is that you happen to break down, you should be covered for free towing services.

   AAA also has really good member benefits. From travel services, to insurance plans, to financial services, they really offer a lot. You can call them up at any time and request free maps of any kind, and they will send them to your home within one week of your order. All of this is a free service that is provided to it's members. You don't even have to pay for the postage and handling. Whether you are at home, or traveling on the road, your AAA *Plus* card can save you money in many ways. I sound like a salesman for AAA, but I am not. I am just a guy who has used his AAA *Plus* card many times over the years to save a lot of money when I was on the road filming movies.

   Below is a link to the main website for AAA:

http://www.aaa-mountainwest.com/products.htm

This website will give you all the information you need to become a member of AAA. Member services are offered online, over the phone, or in person at one of the many AAA offices that are located in every major city in America. You can get the address and directions to any of these locations on their website. Most of these AAA locations have a store inside that sells a variety of books and things related to traveling. Maps and tour guide books are free to all members.

Once again, I have no connection with AAA other than the fact that I am a member. I am not a spokesperson, and I am not shilling for The Auto Club. I am just trying to save you money on your road trip film shoots.

• DIRECTING-

As the Director of your movie it is your responsibility to get your cast and crew to understand your vision. After that, it is up to them to interpret it on film (and DAT tape). You must be very passionate in your delivery so that you let everyone know that you are expecting great things out each one of them. Explain to them that the outcome of your film production depends on the work that you all do as a team for the next couple of weeks. They must understand that while your movie has a very small budget, it has a very large heart. From the principle actors to the people who carry the equipment, one hundred percent effort is expected by all who are involved with the making of your film.

You must know when to wear your Director's hat

While it is necessary to wear many different hats when you make a low budget movie, you must also know the right time and place to wear each particular hat. Before and after filming starts you are most often wearing the hats of Writer and Producer, but when the camera is rolling, you must be all Director.

Your primary duties as Director are; visualize your story through the camera lens, tell your cast and crew what you need from them, and then make sure everyone gives you everything that is necessary to get your film made.

While your cast and crew are executing your plan you should be watching them very closely. You must be aware of the job that each person is doing at all times. If someone is not living up to your standards, then you have to let them know immediately. You cannot be shy about this; the longer you wait the more time and money you will lose. Step right in when necessary, but do it with respect and tact. You must be able to communicate without ruffling feathers.

The Director must also be an Administrator, a Supervisor, and a Diplomat

Be strict, but do not be a tyrant. If you want things to run smoothly; YOU MUST GET ALONG WITH YOUR CAST AND CREW. You must be strong-willed with your vision, but you must also be willing to compromise at certain times with the production process in order to avoid destructive and time-consuming disagreements.

You must always find a way to keep the production process rolling along at a fast pace. Sometimes that means making concessions on your part. Remember, you agreed to give the cast crew a certain amount of creative control so they would agree to work for less than the usual pay. You cannot go back on your word, or you will have a very unhappy cast and crew.

Listen to people who really know their job

If someone in the cast or crew feels strongly about the way they should do their job, then it would be a good idea to listen to them. If their idea sounds good, you should accept it, as long as it does not require any important dialogue or story changes to your film. The fact that you hired this person shows that you believe they know how to do their job well. Keep that in mind when you are having a discussion with them (not an argument) over how something should be filmed. They definitely know their job better than you know it. Let them have their way as long as the ultimate outcome represents your film vision.

Showing Anger is unprofessional behavior

If you encounter a situation where a person in your cast or crew disagrees with you on how something should be filmed it is very important that you do not let any tempers flare up. While you demand a certain degree of passion out of your employees it is important that they keep that passion controlled when a disagreement arises. The people who work on films are artists, and good artists are very passionate about their work, but there is no room for that passion to spillover into anger when you are having discussions with your cast and crew. While *film* is a very artistic medium that requires a certain amount of passion, it is also a very technical medium as well. This technical aspect requires clear heads and calm demeanors to create good work. When people get upset about something, they are usually not thinking very clearly. When anger is included in the process of filmmaking, the result is a poor quality product.

If someone begins to show anger in the course of a discussion it is your job as the Director to calm them down. Do not make the situation worse by showing anger in return. The first thing you should do is remind them that their behavior is very unprofessional. Under no circumstances should you, the Director ever show anger on the set. Anger denotes a loss of control. As the Director of your film you must always be in control.

You will not run into too many situations where you are arguing with cast and crew members if you plan everything out thoroughly ahead of time. These types of costly nightmares can be avoided with the proper amount of location scouting, research, crew meetings, etc... This is true because you can eliminate the unforeseen problems and the need to make decisions on the spot. When you do the proper amount of pre-production work, everyone knows what they are getting into ahead of time, and this makes things run more smoothly. It will also show that you are organized and well prepared, and this makes you look good in the eyes of your cast and crew.

Be resourceful when problems arise

If bad weather forces you to change your plans, then use it to your advantage. You can even incorporate the weather into your storyline if you are clever.

I have a friend who worked on *Jurassic Park* as a second unit cameraman, and he told me stories about what it was like to work on that film. Of course, his favorite story was the one about the hurricane. It is also one of my favorite film production stories of all time.

Steven Spielberg was shooting Jurassic Park on the island of Kauai, in Hawaii, when a sudden unexpected change in the weather occurred that threatened to cause major problems with his shooting schedule. Hurricane Iniki slammed into the island in the middle of filming. This was a very strong hurricane that brought torrential rains and high winds with it. The script called for a warm, tropical location, so quite obviously 120 mile an hour winds and 12 inches of rain was not going to fit in with the storyline. Needless to say, filming was brought to a halt as Spielberg was forced to accept the fact that the approaching storm was not fitting in with his original film vision.

While everyone on the island of Kauai was hunkering down in fear of the approaching storm, Spielberg was thinking of a way to use this potentially deadly storm to his advantage. Although his film production had been blindsided by this unforeseen weather event, Spielberg was determined to keep the ball rolling. Being the resourceful genius that he is, Spielberg decided to add the hurricane to the storyline. The hurricane would now be a character in the movie that threatens to destroy key elements of Jurassic park and cause chaos in the aftermath.

I would love to have been a fly on the wall of Spielberg's meetings during that time so I could have watched a brilliant director in action, making decisions that would make or break the success of his film. As any great Director would do, he took charge of the situation and came up with a brilliant contingency plan that would save his film production.

As the hurricane moved into the area and the heavy rains began to fall, Spielberg resumed filming. He shot scenes in the rain that were originally supposed to be shot with sunny weather. When the weather became too rough to film outside, everyone went back to their hotel rooms to wait it out. Even during the worst part of the hurricane, when people were advised to not leave their hotel rooms, Spielberg had his crew working. His second unit film crew shot spectacular shots of the angry hurricane coming ashore from the relative safety of their hotel windows. A lot of these shots made it into the movie. No need to buy stock footage of a hurricane. They had the real thing already in the can.

The results of these decisions by Spielberg were very beneficial to the movie. The relentless falling rain gave the movie a creepy look, much like it does in a good horror or suspense film. It also added a sense of urgency to the already dangerous situations that the characters in the movie faced. Not only did they have an angry T-Rex to worry about, but they also had an angry Mother Nature as well.

Adding the rain and wind to the storyline also served as powerful symbolism that represented the proverbial raining on a parade. In the movie, Jurassic park was supposed to be an amusement park like Disneyland or Six Flags, with a bright and sunny image. The storm that slammed into the island represented the dousing of a brilliant idea by an unforeseen problem. In the end, it was more than the weather that ruined the dinosaur amusement park, but it served as an effective reinforcement of the theme that mankind cannot control science and nature. As we all know, this film went on to be one of the highest grossing films of all time, and it also received decent reviews from the film critics.

The moral of this story is; when life gives you lemons on a film shoot, make lemonade. Spielberg took a potentially disastrous situation and turned it into a beneficial one. While it is true that Steven Spielberg is one of the best film directors in the history of cinema, and he works on big budget films, he is no different than directors of small films in one aspect; he must make major decisions throughout the film production process that effect the outcome of his film.

The true hallmarks of a great director are their ability to make others understand their vision, and their ability to adapt to unforeseen problems. This is true for all film directors, whether they are famous, or just starting out.

Be very conservative with the use of film stock

While most big film directors have the luxury of shooting every shot in every scene many, many times, directors of smaller films do not have that luxury. Once again, movie film is very expensive, and should be used

PRODUCTION / 151.

frugally when you are shooting your low budget film. While the paramount concern of any director who works on a big studio film is to stay loyal to his creative vision, the director of a low budget movie has to think about the budget first.

A lot of the directors of *big* films will sometimes shoot as many as thirty-five or forty takes of a single shot to get the one that satisfies them. The idea of conserving film is not even an issue on larger film productions. The studio is paying for the film, and they will always give the directors of their films all the film stock they need.

The director of a small film cannot afford to keep shooting until he gets it right. You must take what you can get and then get out. It is very challenging at times to walk away from a shot that you are not one hundred percent happy with, but it is necessary.

Shoot quickly and wait for nothing

The shooting formula that you use to shoot your film is very important. "Run and Gun" is the best name to describe the style of shooting that you must use if you want to get every scene of your movie shot in a short amount of time. This method basically requires you and your outfit to be very mobile, prepared, focused, and fast. As I said, forget everything you have heard about the term "hurry up and wait" regarding the film industry and the way they work on a film set, because it does not apply to the small budget films. When you direct your own film, your motto should be "Always Fast and Efficient".

If you want to save a lot of time, film, and money, your shooting formula should be as follows:

1. Film with a 3:1 shooting ratio (no more than 3 takes for every shot you film).

2. Start with a MASTER SHOT (full shot) for every scene.

   A. Shoot one take of the whole scene with a static Master shot.

   a. If any actors mess up badly on their lines or a crew member makes a major mistake, start the scene again at the point where you left off. Do not start again from the beginning. You can film some close ups and inserts a little later and edit around the stoppage in filming.

   b. Your actors should be told to improvise (ad-lib) if they make a mistake with their lines. You want to do everything you can to impress upon your actors that they must keep the scene going at all costs. This does not mean that they have a free pass to disregard your script. Your actors are expected to read the lines of your script verbatim unless a change has been approved by you.

   Improvising should be done as a last resort, and only to save you time and money. Sometimes, the improvised take you get is better than the one on the script. Some actors just seem to need a little adversity to give you a good performance. You should yell "cut!" only when it is absolutely necessary.

    c. You must film no more than 3 TAKES OF EACH SHOT. Even if you are not happy with the 3 takes you have, you must move on and some how make up for it later in another scene or with a minor rewrite of the script. Most of the time you can rescue a shot that you have been forced to move past by inserting a couple of "add-on" lines into a scene that you film later. Another way to make up for shots that you did not get in the allotted three takes is to "fix it in post". For example; you could record the dialogue on your DAT tape at the end of the day or in the hotel room that night and use it later as voice over for a flashback or cut-away shot when you are doing the editing part of your film. Before you make the time and effort to do this you must decide whether or not that particular dialogue is absolutely essential to your storyline. If it is not, then don't worry about it, and move forward.

B. Shoot another take of the whole scene with a "Steadycam" or "hand-held" master shot.

    a. Tell the DP/Cinematographer/Grip to move about the scene in which he follows the action with a fluid, moving shot.

    b. Refer to a, b & c above.

3. Shoot important CLOSE-UPS and INSERTS after you have filmed your master shots. These shots, along with your two masters will give you a variety of shots to edit your scenes.

Tips for Getting Good Performances from Actors

The best way to get good performances out of your actors is to not pressure them too much. You are only going to rattle them if you apply pressure. An overbearing director will not achieve good results with his actors. They will get flustered, and then they will lose sight of their primary motivation. They will become focused on getting you off their back instead of focusing on the emotions that are required to shoot the scene. Good actors require a calm director to give a good performance.

Avoid Negative Energy

A good film director knows that it is important to make their actors feel relaxed on the set. It is their job to set the tone each day when they are filming. An uptight and pushy director only brings negative energy to the set, and that affects everyone who is working around them. Negative energy is contagious, and when it is spewing out from the person in charge it is not long before everyone on the set is infected. You must always bring positive energy with you when you are working on your film.

If someone is not getting a line, then calmly try to explain to them the way that you would like them to do it. Remind them of the way they did it in rehearsal, and then try it again. If they do not get it in 3 takes, then politely tell them that it is time to move forward, and that you can "fix it in post". There is not enough time or film to spend on any actor who seems to have a sudden mental block of the lines that they knew perfectly well during rehearsals, so do not pressure them. Be passionate with your demands on your actors, but only for three takes of each shot, and then realize that the low budget aspect of your film cannot be ignored. You must move forward after 3 takes.

- **CINEMATOGRAPHY-**

Your DP/Cinematographer/Grip is responsible for the way your story will look on film. While your main job as a Director is to explain your vision to your cast and crew, it is the DP/Cinematographer/Grip's job to make that vision come alive on celluloid. Once you have explained to them what you want, it is up to them to decide on what lighting you will need, what time of day would be the best time to shoot, or anything else that would be needed to achieve the results you desire.

Be flexible

The process of making a movie involves input from many different creative types. It is a collaborative effort to be sure, and no film gets made without several changes being made to the original vision of the Producer/Director/Writer. The worst thing you could do is refuse to accept any changes to your directions. If the cast and crew feel that you have gone back on your word to give them creative control with their jobs, then you will have a mutiny on your hands. They could abandon you and your film project before the shooting is finished, and this would be a disaster. You will have to start your hiring process all over again, and that will cost you a lot of time and money.

   You must place a certain amount of trust in the DP/Cinematographer/Grip after you agree to hire them to shoot your film. Filmmaking is one of the only forms of art that requires more than one artist to produce a product. The chance to have creative freedom on a film is most likely the reason why they signed on with your project, so make sure you do not smother them with stipulations and control. Do not try to tell them how to do their job, for it will only lead to resentment of you and unwanted friction on the set. If you feel strongly about shooting something in a particular way, give suggestions, not orders.

   If the DP/Cinematographer/Grip disagrees with you on something, then make sure that you hear them out before you discount their ideas. As I said earlier; they are the one who specializes in cinematography, not you. Most of the time, their way of doing it is the best way. You should not worry too much about the DP/Cinematographer/Grip injecting a little of their own creative touch as long as the core of your vision is represented in the dailies you receive after each film shoot. You must work very closely with this person throughout your film production or you may get a completely different "look" than the one you envisioned. Let them add their own ideas, but do not let them change the way you intended your film to appear on the screen. You must learn to compromise without abandoning your vision.

Steadycam is good

Hiring a DP/Cinematographer/Grip with a "Steadycam" package is a good idea. Shooting most of your scenes with a Steadycam operator saves you a lot of time and allows you to be versatile. For example; if you have a party scene or a group shot to film, it is a lot less time-consuming to have the camera roll for the entire scene while following the action than it is to stop down and shoot several different shots for each piece of dialogue. A good Steadycam operator can move around a scene so smoothly that the audience does not even notice the movement. The viewer can feel like they are a character that is floating around the scenes as they watch your story unfold up close and personal, instead of witnessing it from afar.

Once again, it is extremely important that all your actors have their lines memorized before you begin shooting, or the Steadycam method is no cheaper to use than the static, multiple set-up, tripod method. You will still use the tripod method to shoot such things as extreme close-ups, inserts, and wide shots, but the majority of your film should be shot using the mobile Steadycam method.

Steadycam packages are not cheap to purchase, but that's okay, because you don't need to buy one. Instead, you can rent one with a DP/Cinematographer included, and all for a very reasonable price.

In most of the major cities of the United States there are a lot of talented DP/Cinematographers who have done a few small films, but would like to get work on big studio films. They go out and spend tens of thousands of dollars on a Steadycam package with the idea in mind that the jobs will find *them* if they invest in state of the art equipment.

Unfortunately for *them*, this does not happen due to the fact that every camera person in town now has a Steadycam package and they are all competing for the same jobs. On top of that, there are the nepotism and "connections" factors that make it hard in the first place to break into the film business "big time". What this means is that there are a lot of DP/Cinematographers with Steadycam packages who are desperate to put their talent and equipment to work, even if it means working at a substantially discounted rate. They need to make any money they can to pay off the loans they took out to buy the equipment, and they also want to build their "reels". This is where you can benefit. You can get one of these talented DP/Cinematographers to work on your film with their Steadycam package, and you only have to pay them what your meager budget permits.

While it would seem like it is expensive to hire a camera person with a Steadycam package, this really is not the case. To find a DP/Cinematographer with a Steadycam package; refer to my section titled Finding a Good, Affordable Crew.

If you cannot find an affordable Steadycam operator, then go with the standard "hand-held" method. Just make sure that the DP/Cinematographer/Grip you hire is experienced with doing hand-held filming or your shots will be too shaky. This can give your audience a headache trying to follow the action, and needless to say, this will not win you any favorable reviews.

You must take control of your exposed film

At the end of each filming day it is imperative that you get every can of film that your DP/Cinematographer/Grip shot that day. Do not assume that they will keep all of your film rolls together during a week long shoot and then give them all to you at the end of the week.

Things can happen; the DP/Cinematographer/Grip is overworked and tired, everyone is in a hurry to get back to their hotel/motel rooms and rest, then the next thing you know is you are missing the most important roll of your movie. This actually happened to me once, but it will never happen again. I lost the most important roll of my movie once, and to this day I am kicking myself for not taking that roll at the end of the day. It was a roll from the climax scene of a movie I made called *Black Mountain Way*. The two main characters were fighting to the death, and the outcome of the movie was to be decided in this scene. I shot it in the Sierra Mountains near the town of Bridgeport, in California. The whole shoot went great. At the end of a long day of filming we were all exhausted, so we hurriedly packed up and drove to our hotel rooms. I *assumed* that the DP/Cinematographer/Grip had all the rolls of film we shot that day safely stored in his hotel room that night, but I was wrong. The next day I asked him for the rolls we shot the day before, and that is when my nightmare began.

When we tallied up the cans of film, we realized that one was missing. Some how the best roll had mysteriously disappeared. The worst part about it was that it I could not film the scene again, for everyone involved had commitments pending and needed to drive home the same day we realized the roll was missing. My anxiety level was

PRODUCTION   /   160.

through the roof that day as I realized that without that roll of film, my movie made no sense.

Everyone but me drove home that day. I stayed behind another day to scour the area where we were filming the day before, but I never did find that roll of film. I even had to pay for an extra day of equipment rental. One thing became very clear to me on that long, hot, beautiful drive home through the Owens Valley on that desert highway with the Sierra Mountains serving as a backdrop; I will never again let my film rolls out of my sight when I am on film shoots. Even when they are in the lab they are not one hundred percent safe, as I also learned the hard way. I will touch on that nightmare subject in the Post- Production section. It took me one lost roll of film on a film shoot and two lost rolls at film labs to realize that my film is never really safe until it has been transferred to video or DVD.

Your exposed cans of film are your precious vision on celluloid, and you should not trust them in the hands of anyone but yourself until you drop them off at the film lab for processing. Once the filming day is over, and your film is in the can, you must take charge of it. If possible, you should go directly to the film lab and drop off your film cans right after each film shoot. The less time you have that film in your hands undeveloped, the less time you have to worry about it getting damaged or compromised by some unfortunate event.

As for the film lab, there is not much you can do about them losing your rolls of film. Once you drop it off at the lab, your film is in the hands of the employees who work at that lab. Don't get me wrong. I have dropped off thousands of rolls of film at film labs during the twenty years that I have been making movies, and I have only had two rolls lost. It does not happen very often with any good film labs.

Most film lab employees treat your film as carefully as you treat it yourself, but it only takes that one time where they suddenly just don't care, and they are in charge of your film. This is when you get a lost roll of film, and an independent filmmaker who can't believe his bad luck. In my case, it was two times. The first time it happened to me I was heinously shunned by the company who lost my roll of film. Instead of acknowledging their mistake and trying to make up for it, they chose to hide behind the small writing on the form I signed when I dropped off the film.

The second time a film lab lost one of my rolls of film was a much different experience than the first one. It happened to me was at a different film lab, and they handled it much better. I received a sincere apology, and I was also compensated sufficiently with free lab services. They were both nice gestures, but they didn't bring back my very important roll of film. I will explain more about these incidents later, but my message is that you must watch your film like a hawk while you are in the midst of filming, and you should choose your film labs carefully before you drop off those rolls of film.

Detailed labeling is important

Make sure that each can of film is labeled correctly when you are filming. There must also be a production note sheet with every can of film that has detailed information on it. These sheets must include specific information about everything that is on each particular role (roll numbers, scene numbers, number of takes, specific shots, location, date, etc...). You will keep these sheets after you drop your film off at the lab, and use them as a reference any time you have a question about what scenes are on which rolls. You will bring them with you when you screen your *dailies*.

Labeling is usually the job of the Focus Puller/Camera Assistant/Grip, but sometimes the DP/Cinematographer/Grip will perform this task. Make sure you tell this person that you are a stickler for details when it comes to labeling film cans, and tell the Focus Puller/Camera Assistant/Grip as well.

Make sure your digital slates are legible

Another thing that you should mention to the DP/Cinematographer/Grip at the beginning of your film shoots is to make sure they film a good, clear close up shot of the digital slate when you slate your shots. Sometimes they can get lazy, or sometimes they are just in a hurry to shoot and get out of a location. For whatever reason, they sometimes shoot a half-hearted effort on your film slates that leaves you with red numbers that you cannot read because they are too far away or out of focus. If the glowing red numbers on the digital "smart" slate are not legible, then it will be a lot harder for you to sync your picture up with your sound. As in most cases, the hard way is going to cost you a lot more money than the easy way.

- **SOUND-**

PRODUCTION / 163.

    This is one aspect of filmmaking where the playing field is pretty much level for everyone in the game. Nowadays, sound equipment is relatively inexpensive to buy. The best news of all is that the low end models of sound equipment are capable of giving you sound quality that is comparable to the quality you will get from expensive equipment that is used by the sound people who work on the big studio films.

    It is a lot cheaper than it used to be to get yourself set up with the equipment you need to be a Soundman (person). There are more sound people looking for work in the film business than ever before, and they are not nearly as expensive to hire as they used to be.

    If you hire a quality Soundman (person) with good equipment who takes their job seriously, then you can have almost the same quality sound as any big movie that you see in the major theaters. The best part about is that you will not have to pay a lot of money like the big studios do. This was not the case only a couple of decades ago, due to the high costs of buying sound equipment. It is much different these days. Things have changed dramatically since the invention of digital sound. The old reel-to-reel *Nagra* tape recorders that are big, temperamental, and expensive, are no longer the only way to get good quality sound recorded for your film. Although they do give excellent quality sound recordings, Nagras are a burden to carry around on location. They do not work well for your "run and gun" shooting style. It is much easier for your sound person to carry around a small DAT (digital audio tape) recorder. Nowadays, sound equipment is smaller, better quality, and more affordable than ever before, and this means that you can have good quality sound for your film at a price that suits your miniscule budget.

Good sound is very important

Good quality sound can make up for a compromised visual look that tends to come with a small film budget. Film festival judges and film audiences will tolerate almost any level of production value when it comes to the visual part of a film, but they will not put up with poor quality sound. People tend to underestimate the importance of sound on a film, but it is actually more important than the visuals when it comes to production value. If you have excellent quality sound for your film, viewers tend to overlook other not so excellent technical aspects.

Another thing to consider regarding digital audio is the fact that it is a lot easier to pop DAT tapes (digital audio tapes) in and out of your recording unit than it is to change reel-to-reel tapes on a Nagra unit. The whole process of using a DAT recorder is just faster, easier, and cheaper than using a Nagra recorder and these are very important factors when you are making a movie with a very, very, low budget.

Some would argue that DAT tape recordings do not sound quite as good as the high quality reel-to-reel tape recordings do, but most of these people would agree that the difference is not that much. If you hire competent sound people with good DAT equipment to do the sound for your movie, the average audience member will not be able to tell the difference.

PRODUCTION   /   165.

There are a lot of good sound people out there who have bought a DAT recording package, and are just aching to work on a film like yours so they can use their equipment and build their resume. Just like everyone else you hire to work on your film, they are willing to work for a lot less than the industry standard pay in order to get experience. All you have to do is search for them at the right places.

To find them you need to go to places where the Sound People hangout, just like you did when you were looking for your DP/Cinematographer/Grip. This means going to the sound rental houses where they rent sound equipment packages to people who make movies. Talk to the people at the desk; ask them if they know of any affordable sound people who have their own DAT packages and might like to work on a film that has a very, very, low budget.

The audio of your low budget film does not have to sound like it did not cost much money. If you do your homework in the hiring process you should be able to find a really good sound person (and boom operator). For details on how to find these kinds of people see the section on *finding a good, affordable crew.*

Let your Sound People worry about sound

You should not worry too much about the sound part of your film once filming starts. You will have your hands full with the visual aspects. A good two person sound duo can operate almost direction-free when you are filming. They know their objective and they can move along with the rest of your outfit almost undetected like a pilot fish on the side of a humpback whale.

PRODUCTION   /   166.

You can let your sound people have a little looser chain than the visual people.

   There is not much for you to do in terms of hands on sound work during the filming process, so once again, do not be afraid to give your Soundman (person) creative control. You must stress to this person at the beginning of your shoots that you are counting on them to give you good, clear, professional sounding audio for every scene that is filmed. After that, it is up to them to just do the job that you are paying them to do. Your creative input in terms of sound effort on your film project will happen later in the post-production process when you will be working closely with your Sound Designer/Mixer.

   You will get to do fun and exiting stuff that includes such things as voice over and *foley* sound effects. During filming, the sound recording responsibility is all in the hands of your Soundman (person) and his Boom Operator/Audio Assistant/Grip.

Ask to hear samples of sound when you are filming

   While it is true that you can give your sound people a lot of leeway, it is still important that you monitor their work while you are filming. After all, sound is a very big part of the production value of your film, so it is important that you do a quality check every once in a while. Don't be afraid to ask your sound person to cue up and play back a sound bite that you are really wondering about. Just make sure you do it during a period of down time when you are not filming. You should not stop the rapid flow of your well-oiled film unit every time you get a curious thought about the way something might or might not have been recorded. Needless to say, this will cost you money in wasted time. Wait for a lull in the filming process before you make any inquiries about audio.

A good time to do your sound checks is when your DP/Cinematographer/Grip is changing the film in the camera. This process usually takes a few minutes, which is more than enough time to cue up a digital sound bite, put the headphones on and then hear it.

Even if you are not wondering about any particular sound recording it is a good idea to ask your Soundman (person) every once in a while to playback samples of the recordings they just made. This will give you peace of mind later on when you are going over in your mind the things that you shot that day. It is a good feeling to know when you lay down at night that the sound recorded for your film is high quality stuff. This will only improve the chances that your film will be a success.

Use wireless microphones

It is a good idea to use wireless lavalier microphones for your actors when ever it is possible. These are the small microphones you see clipped to the tie or lapel of news reporters and anchor people on television when they are reporting the news. Sound people in the film business use the same kind of microphones, but the difference is; they make sure the audience cannot see them.

Most sound people who work on location have a variety of wireless microphones in their sound packages. These collections usually include anything from hand-mikes to tiny flesh-tone lavaliers that can be taped to the neck of an actor, or attached inside the collar with a "vampire clip" (a clip with two small pins on it that look like vampire fangs). These microphones are especially useful in any situation where you do not want to draw attention to the fact that you are filming a movie. You can conceal them well and get great audio at any location. The sight of a person holding a boom microphone encased in a "zeppelin" with a furry "dead cat" wind screen on it tends to catch people's attention. Wireless mikes are more indiscreet, and will not draw a crowd when you are filming.

Using wireless lavalier microphones for your actors eliminates the chance of boom operator error that can result in such things as the sound being too faint on some dialogue. This usually happens when the person holding the boom does not have the microphone close enough to the subject that was speaking at that time.

Always record a backup track on channel 2

In addition to having all of your principal actors miked up with concealed wireless microphones, it is a good idea to tell your Soundman (person) to record the boom microphone or a wireless hand mike on channel 2 of their DAT recorder. This way you will have another track to use if one of your actor's wireless microphones goes down. You never know when you will lose a piece of sound due to a dead microphone battery or a malfunction in the placement, so it is good to have two tracks to choose from.

PRODUCTION / 169.

Most sound people will automatically do this, but you should double check just to make sure.

Be stealthy with your microphones

   If you are shooting in a crowded public place and you are trying to be stealthy with your filming, it is a lot easier to have your Boom Operator/Audio Assistant/Grip move through the crowd holding a small wireless hand-microphone than it is to carry a large "shotgun" mike on a "boom-pole". A hand mike is not *omni directional*, and it may not give you quite as good of sound quality as a shotgun microphone, but it is much less conspicuous. The slight difference in quality does not matter at all because this will more than likely only be used as your *natural sound* and emergency back-up track.

Do not pay more for the use of wireless microphones

   Wireless microphones cost a lot to buy, and they are a bit more complex to use than a boom microphone with a "hardwire" cable attached right to the DAT recorder. Sometimes sound people will cite this fact as a reason to charge a higher rate for including the use of wireless microphones on a film job. While they may have a point, that kind of charge typically should not apply to a client such as yourself (with very little money). That is a fee that most sound people agree to waive when they work on small budget films. They usually reserve those premium fees for the higher paying clients. Make sure that the person you hire includes the use of these types of mikes with your payment agreement. This must be discussed during the hiring process. You do not want any hidden costs popping up during your production process, so make sure that wireless microphones are part of your deal when you draw up the release form for your Soundman (person). Be sure they are aware of this stipulation before they sign their release form. If they do not agree to this deal, then tell them the deal is off and call some of the other sound people that sent you their resumes and CDs.

Your Soundman (person) must be diligent with time code and log sheets

When your sound person is recording the sound on your movie with their DAT recorder it is very important that they log accurate time code numbers for each and every shot. This is a very important part of the DAT recording process. These are the numbers that your sound technician depends on when you are syncing up the sound for your film "dailies". Any incorrect time code logging will cause expensive delays in the sound syncing process. This is because the technician has to search for the correct time code numbers manually instead of simply reading a number on the log sheet and going right to the desired location on the tape. Of course, while they are wasting time searching for the right time code numbers they are still on your dollar. As with everything else that has to do with spending money on your film you want to spend as little time as possible with anyone that charges by the hour, especially when you are paying them hundreds of dollars per hour.

Any good Soundman (person) understands the importance of logging every take accurately, and they are usually very diligent about logging the correct time code when they are recording sound. Just make sure you stress to this person before filming begins the importance of having your time code loggings correct for every take of every shot

Take charge of your DAT tapes at the end of the day

Just as you do with your rolls of film when filming ends, you need to get every DAT tape at the end of all film shoots, every day. They must also be labeled carefully, with all the necessary details included. Anything that your Soundman (person) records during your shoots needs to go with the cans of film that were used that day. It is a good idea to put these items in a black film bag or a thick, black duffle bag. You must keep that bag in a cool, dry place, and guard it with your life until you your film has been developed and your dailies have been synced up with sound. I will discuss this very important issue in more detail in the next few pages.

• PROPS, COSTUMES, AND SPECIAL EFFECTS-

In any movie other than a low budget movie, these three things would be three different jobs for three different people. However, with your film production, all of these jobs go to one person. As with everyone else you hire, your Props/Costume/Special Effects person must do the job of at least three people and get paid a lot less than they are worth. The good news for the person you hire for this job is that your carefully written low budget script does not require very much work regarding props, costumes, and special effects. The strength of your film is in it's storyline and the performances of your actors, not in it's production value. Any props, costumes, and special effects that are required will be very basic, and will not require a lot of work.

Keep your props, costumes, and special effects materials well organized and clearly labeled

Props, costumes, and special effects materials should be stored in clear, plastic containers. All the containers must have labels that include detailed information about what scene the contents inside will be used for, what actor will use them, as well as the location they will be used at, etc.... This is part of your pre-production phase, so everything should be ready to go when you start filming. Everything must be neatly organized and easy to access so there are absolutely no delays in the filming process when something is needed. This packaging and labeling is your responsibility. It should be done long before filming begins.

You **must acquire, store, and label all props, costumes, and special effects materials yourself**

You will provide all of the props, costumes, and materials for the special effects in your film. You are the one who is in charge of all these items before and after a film shoot. You will keep all of the containers in your vehicle, and hand them over to the Props/Costumes/Special Effects person each day before the filming begins. The reason you do this is to ensure that you will still have all the props, costumes, and special effects materials in your possession if the person you hire to do this job suddenly decides to abandon you in the middle of a film shoot (it happens). You should keep these items in your possession, and hand them out at the beginning of each day. Once the work day begins, your Props/Costume/Special Effects person is in charge of these items, and they must promptly provide each item when it is needed.

Makeup for your actors is not mandatory

You do not have to worry too much about make-up for your actors. Make-up should be used sparingly, if at all. You are going for the "natural" look with your movie, so you do not need much make-up. If any actors prefer to wear make-up, then they must buy their own, and apply it themselves before the work day begins. You need to make it clear to your actors beforehand that there will be no time allotted for applying makeup once the filming day begins. Any special effects make-up for things like blood, bruises, or scars will be provided by you, and applied by your Props/Costume/Special Effects person when needed. You can buy materials for fake blood, bruises, and scars at any costume/party shop.

As for special effects, well, they just are not that special when you do not have a big budget to accommodate them. That is why you want to keep them very basic and very few in terms of numbers.

As with the props and costumes, you must buy any materials necessary for special effects ahead of time and give them to your Props/Costume/Special Effects person just before each day of filming begins. Any time a special effect is needed when you are filming, it is the job of this person to produce the necessary materials, and make it happen. You should discuss all of their responsibilities during crew meetings (both in the pre-production phase and

PRODUCTION   /   174.

before every shoot) so they can be prepared for any task that you will require them to perform. Even when you are using the most basic props, costumes, and special effects for a film, it requires thorough planning ahead of time to be successful. Otherwise, there could be costly delays as your whole cast and crew waits for you to figure out how to do something or to find something that you "misplaced".

• STORAGE OF EXPOSED FILM AND DAT TAPES-

This is an EXTREMELY IMPORTANT ISSUE. Improper handling and storage of your exposed roles of film and your used DAT tapes during and after the filming process can ruin all of the hard work that you and your outfit put into your film production. While it is the responsibility of the DP/Cinematographer/Grip and your Soundman (person) to properly handle your roles of film and DAT tapes while you are filming, as I stated earlier, when the filming stops for the day, it is your responsibility to acquire them.

Your exposed film and DAT tape Masters should never leave your sight

You should keep your DAT tapes and rolls of film together, along with the log sheets and labels. This is a very important issue when you are filming your movie. If you lose or damage any one of these items, your film will be severely compromised, you will suffer unspeakable mental anguish, and you will look like an idiot before your cast and crew. Treat these items as if they were something you cannot live without, like oxygen and water, or you will be asking for trouble.

   You can buy a bag or a container for transporting film at any camera shop, or you can do what I do, and spend a fraction of the money. I always seal my cans of film and DAT tapes in large Ziploc bags, and then I put them in brown paper bags. After that I put the bags in a heavy duty black duffle bag ($10 at Wal-Mart) for safe keeping.

   If you are shooting on location, that black duffle bag should never leave your sight. It should be kept in the shade at all times, where you can see it. Never leave your bag uncovered or unprotected when the sun is up in the sky. You should always protect this bag from prolonged exposure to the sun when you are filming, as well as from any natural elements such as dirt, sand, or water. You should also protect it when you are in transit to and from the shooting locations.

   When you finish filming for the day, that bag with your precious film and DAT tapes inside should not leave your sight until you close your eyes and go to sleep in your bed. Even then it will be on the floor next to your bed where you can see it in case you wake up in the middle of the night after having a nightmare that your bag was slowly sinking into a pool of red-hot molten lava (I had that dream once). Like I said, you won't be able to rest completely until your film has been transferred to video or DVD and the sound has been synced up.

Protect your film and DAT bag while at home or in a hotel room

You should keep this bag away from the kitchen, the laundry room and the bathroom when you are in a hotel room or at your home. These places have a lot of water, which translates into a lot of possibilities for damage to your film and DAT tapes. For instance, it would not be a good idea to put this bag in a cabinet next to a washing machine or a laundry room sink. If the machine malfunctions and overflows it could ruin your film.

Never leave the bag next to a fish tank or a fountain. One moderate earthquake could knock the tank or fountain over and soak your bag. You should also never leave your black duffle bag under a table where there are glasses or bottles that have liquids of any kind in them.

Drop your film off at the lab as soon as possible

As I mentioned earlier, it is a good idea to drop your exposed rolls of film off at the film lab every day after each shoot, if this is possible. If you just finished up a week long shoot out on location somewhere, then by all means, DROP YOUR FILM OFF IMMEDIATELY at the film lab. Film is way too delicate of a substance to hold on to any longer than you have too, so the very same day that you arrive home from shooting, you need to stop by the film lab and drop off your precious cans of film before you go home and sleep for three days straight. As I said before, choose your film lab carefully. It must be a lab that has a very good reputation in the film industry, and one that you trust with your rolls of film. You may get a little bit of a discount on the rates for their services if you tell the lab that you are working with a very small budget, but don't expect much of a break. They all charge by the foot, and the prices are pretty standard among the well-established film labs.

Beware of any lab that offers a price that is substantially lower than any of the other places you checked, for it probably means that they are a new lab that is trying to attract customers. They may prove to be a good lab, but you do not want to be their guinea pig with your film project.

If you have not yet established a relationship with a good film lab, then talk to other people who work in the film industry and ask them which labs are the best ones to use. You can ask any person at any of the film equipment rental houses you go to, and they will tell you which ones are the best. There are usually a handful of top quality film labs in every major city, and those are the ones you should use for your film lab services.

Quality is your primary concern with film labs

Cheaper is not better when it comes to film labs. You only get one chance to develop film, and the quality of your movie rides heavily on how your film is processed. I have tried many different labs over the years and I have found that with this particular service you really must pay the industry standard prices to receive good quality work. There will be no bargaining for the best prices like with the other services you receive in the course of making your movie. Quality should be your primary concern when it comes to choosing a film lab, not price.

You are much more important than you think in the eyes of a film lab

While you are at the film lab you will see all sorts of people dropping off film at the counter. The clientele at these labs ranges from film students with a couple rolls of film in their hands, to film studio couriers with large boxes that are full of exposed film. The interesting thing is that they all get treated the same.

Although your movie seems small compared to the big studio films, there is no need for you to have an inferiority complex. You are more important than you think to these film labs. Even the best film labs will treat you pretty well, even though you are a small time filmmaker. This is because they want to establish a relationship and get you to use their lab for future projects.

There are a lot more independent films made each year than big studio films. Almost everyone who works in the film industry depends on these "small" films for income. If these labs treated small time filmmakers badly, they would not only be jeopardizing a major part of their current income, but they could also be jeopardizing their reputation in the film industry. This could hurt them in the short term and in the long term as well. As I said, small time filmmakers sometimes turn into big time filmmakers, and they usually remember the film labs that treated them right or wrong on the way up

Your film lab must offer free screenings

PRODUCTION   /   179.

   Make sure that you choose a film lab that has screening rooms where you can see your film "dailies" after they are developed. Be sure that this service is included at no extra cost to you. When you drop off your film at the lab, tell the person at the front desk that you want "processing" and "one light work print" for every roll. You will use these prints later on to see your *dailies*, and to cut your "*work print*".

Keep your DAT tapes and log sheets

   Do not drop off your DAT tapes and log sheets with the film. When you are finished filming your movie, you should bring these items home and store them in the safest place you have in your house where they can stay until your film is ready to be synced up with sound.

   After you have finished filming, your film is in the lab, and your DAT tapes are safely stored away, *then* you can turn off the ringer on your phone, turn down the volume on your answering machine, place aluminum foil over your windows, crawl into your bed and sleep like a grizzly bear hibernating during a Siberian winter.

8

Post-Production

After the filming process is over and you finally wake up from your much needed three day slumber, it is time to put the pieces of your puzzle together and make a film. The post-production phase is the part of the film making process where it all comes together, and your film vision becomes complete. It is the part where you finally get to see the fruits of your efforts.

The first thing you must understand when you are doing the post-production phase on a low budget movie is that your *bells and whistles* are going to be severely limited by your miniscule budget. The idea here is to simply put your story together on film with the minimum technical requirements. You are not to trying to create *eye candy*.

The final product you will be striving for is a 16mm film print with an optical sound track on the side of the film. This print(s) will be sent to various film festivals where it will be projected up on "the big screen" (if they decide to show your film). This print will be made from the final edit (master) of your 16mm film negative, and a DAT or CD of the final sound mix that you get from your Sound Designer/Mixer.

During the early days of the 20th century when the film industry was in it's infancy, the post-production part of making a movie was a very simple process. It basically involved cutting film and putting the pieces together by hand with tape or glue. Special effects in those days were not quite as *special* as they are nowadays. The studios did not have the luxury of relying on technology to sell their product, so they had to rely on the creative types of that time to tell good stories.

The big studio pioneers of that era saw the film industry as an opportunity to get in on the ground floor of something big. They realized that this new film industry thing was all about the marriage of technology and the art of story telling. If they wanted to get in on the action, they would have to collaborate with artists who tell good stories.

People like D.W Griffith and Mary Pickford were well aware of the fact that film technology was very limited in those days, but it did not matter to them. They were just happy to be able to tell their stories to millions of people.

While making money was the primary concern of the studios in the early days, for the *film artist*, it was all about getting your story put on film. They had a genuine desire to create films that told interesting, and sometimes important stories (I.E: D.W Griffith's *Birth of a Nation)*. The people who made movies in the early days relied on good stories and strong performances to sell movie tickets, not production value. Filmmaking technology was very basic, even crude by today's standards, but nonetheless, they managed to tell wonderful stories with film, and make a lot of money at the same time.

To make a low budget film you must think like they did in the early days of filmmaking

Making a low budget movie these days is like being transported back in time to the early days of filmmaking. When you are technologically limited by your budget, you are forced to go back to the basics to get your film made. You must favor substance over style if you want to succeed. If you provide a good story, your audiences will not be too concerned about the lack of production value. After all, the film industry was originally built on substance, not style. The people who went to see films in the early days of the film industry went to the theaters to see a good story unfold on the screen, not for the (not so) special effects.

The film audiences of today are no different than they were in the past. While most people *like* a movie with good special effects, everyone *loves* a movie with a good story. If the big studios could figure out a fool-proof method of picking good stories that everyone will *love,* they could make an enormous amount of profit on every film they make. Unfortunately for them, picking a winning script is a very difficult task. If they had the magic formula for picking a winning script, they would not bother to spend millions of dollars on the production values of their films. Scripts cost a lot less than special effects. With lower production costs, their profits would be substantial.

Just get your story out there for everyone to see

Try as they might, the powerful studio executives will never have a monopoly on good story-telling. That is why the people who make small films today still have a chance to be successful in an industry that is dominated by big film studios. "Who you know" in the film industry is very important these days if you want to "break in", but there is one thing that is more important than that; a good script. If you have a great story, your film will succeed without the help of nepotism, a big budget, or post-production *bells and whistles*. All you have to do is put your story on 16mm film, get it in some film festivals, and let the movie-going public decide if it is a good story or not. If they like it, you are in business. The distributors will come running to find you and make a deal to distribute your film.

   Post-production costs were relatively small in the early days of filmmaking. The technology for *bells and whistles* was not very advanced yet. There was not very much work to do other than editing film, syncing sound, and adding music. The entire process only took a few days to complete.

   Today, it is a much different story. Now that film making technology has become highly advanced, studios tend to rely on the production value of films to be successful. They spend millions of dollars on post-production costs for expensive, labor-intensive things such as computer generated special effects, custom sound design, and large orchestras for music. *Lara Croft: Tomb Raider (2001)* and *The Matrix Revolutions (2004)* are a couple of examples of these kind of movies. They are more like video games than they are films. These big budget films that the major studios release each year during the summer and Christmas seasons are made with the idea in mind that the audio-visual experience is more important than the story. Despite the fact that these films lack a storyline, they still pack the theaters when they are released.

The studios know that they do not need to rely on a good story and strong performances to make money with a film. Instead they spend a major part of their big budgets on post-productions costs that will give them a product that is quite simply *eye candy*. Impressive visuals and sound are the only things they need. Most times they make millions of dollars back in profits.

Sometimes a big studio gets lucky and happens to choose a good script to go along with one of their multi-million dollar budget movies. When they add a good story to a film that has a high production value and slick packaging, that film usually breaks box-office records. The irony of it all is that the script is usually the least expensive part of making these record breaking films, but it is the main reason these films are such a big success.

My point is that a good script has more value than all the special effects in the world, and you should not be discouraged because you do not have a lot of money to spend on post-production services for your film. The fact that your film is a well-written, character-driven story makes up for your lack of production value. Film festival judges and other members of your target audience are usually willing to overlook certain deficiencies in the production value, as long as you provide them with an interesting, entertaining story.

Sick to the basics with your post-production phase

There is impressive technology out there these days that is available to enhance the production value of your film in the post-production process. Unfortunately, this technology does not concern you, because you cannot afford to use it when you are making a movie with a very, very low budget. You must stick to the basics in every way. There will be no green screen composites, no computer generated images, and no elaborate sound effects. If you were editing your film Master digitally you would be able to take advantage of some of the impressive editing software that is available for your home computer, but as I said earlier; if you want to be in the game at the film festivals, you have to edit on film. You could edit digitally and then transfer your completed master to a film negative, but that is just way too expensive to do with a small budget film.

Aside from some slight color and exposure corrections, you will not be making many changes to your film images during the post-production process. What you see when you screen your *dailies* is pretty much what you get.

Your film does not necessarily have to look and sound like a low budget film

Just because your movie has a very small budget, this does not mean that it has to look and sound like it does. You can get good quality post-production work that can make your film look and sound very good, and you do not have to spend a lot of money in the process. As with all the other aspects of the film industry, there are a lot of talented post-production people out there who will work on your film for a lot less money than they are worth, either to get more experience, supplement their income, build their *demo reels*, or for all of the above reasons. Just like with all the other people you hire to work on your film, you just need to find them, and then bargain for a good deal.

Websites that offer information about people and places that do post-production work for independent films:

- http://www.la411.com/

- http://www.ny411.com/

- http://www.dirtcheaprentals.com/

- http://www.mandy.com/

- http://www.uniquefilms.com/

To find good deals on post production work you can visit these websites and look for post-production people/houses that work in your area. There are plenty of people and places that do good work at decent prices. Most of them are very familiar with the independent film scene and the budget constraints that are associated with it.

When you are deciding on which people to hire you should use the same criteria that I laid out in the section about finding a good, affordable crew. When you are negotiating with people, just explain your situation and proceed to bargain for the best prices you can get from them.

Your biggest concern with the post-production phase of your movie is making sure that you do not run out of

POST-PRODUCTION   /   187.

money before the process is complete. You must be extra diligent in your efforts to find good quality work that fits your small budget. You only have $10-15,000 (depending on whether or not you use your travel budget money) and you better use it wisely.

- **SCREENING YOUR DAILIES-**

The first thing you need to do is see your footage. This can be a touch and go situation that includes emotions that range from unbridled jubilation and excitement, to complete disappointment and shock. The mood is determined by the outcome of your footage. Hopefully, most of your footage will come out looking nicely exposed, and clear as can be, with all rolls present and accounted for.

As I mentioned earlier, I have had two really bad experiences over the years with film labs losing rolls of my film. However, when I think about the number rolls that I have dropped off at labs over the years to get developed, two rolls really is not that many. Even so, that did not make me feel any better when I realized that all the planning and hard work that was required to film those rolls was just wasted time and effort, not to mention the fact that each roll that is filmed is a vital piece of a puzzle, and losing one piece means that the puzzle will never be complete. Losing those two rolls of film was very painful, and I can only hope it never happens to you. It is like losing a piece of yourself.

I actually went to small claims court the first time a lab lost one of my rolls of film. I tried to sue the lab for the maximum amount allowed by law ($3000 at that time). I went to court and poured my heart out to the judge as I told him how much work was involved with the roll of film that was lost, and how much that roll meant to me as a filmmaker. I was naive enough to think that the judge would feel my pain. He did not.

The legal representative for the owner of the film lab sat there silent as I pleaded my case to the judge. After I was through talking, it was his turn to present his defense. Looking very much like a lawyer, he stood up and produced a copy of the document I signed when I dropped off my rolls of film at the film lab. He gave it to the judge and showed him the part at the bottom of the page that basically releases them from any responsibility for lost or damaged film. I had signed this document with a second nature wave of the hand, and I never even bothered to read the fine print (does anyone?). It was an easy decision for that judge. Needless to say, I lost the case.

You should always maintain a good relationship with your film lab

If a film lab happens to lose or damage any of your rolls of film, there really is not much that you can do about it. There is always some little writing at the bottom of the page you signed when you dropped off your film that says they are not responsible for such things. As horrifying as it sounds to have one of your rolls of film lost at the hands of a careless film lab employee, in reality, it is rare that any reputable film lab will lose or damage your film.

POST-PRODUCTION   /   189.

If this type of thing happens to you, the best thing to do is to play the roll of a person who is very disappointed, but not necessarily angry. Getting angry will only force the film lab to refer to the legal-ease at the bottom of the document you signed when you dropped off your film, and you most certainly will lose if that happens. Remember, you did choose this lab because it has a good reputation in the film industry, and you do not want to have a sour relationship with the best film lab in your town over one lost roll of film (hopefully only one). The chances of them losing another roll of your film are very small. It would be like getting hit by lightning twice.

The best thing to do if a film lab happens to lose or damage any of your rolls of film is forget about the lost rolls of film. They are probably never going to be found by anyone, and there is nobody legally responsible to compensate you for your loss.

After you get over the initial shock of losing a piece of your film vision, you should try and get what you can out of the film lab in the way of free lab services. Tell them that you have you have lost a lot of money because of this incident, and your film project is going to be incomplete until you can re-shoot the scenes that were lost, *if* you can re-shoot them. Also, tell them that you feel they should compensate you with some free lab services as a good-faith gesture. Complain, but do not threaten. If you do not act angry towards them, and you play the role of the wounded party, then most labs will agree to compensate you with a reasonable amount of free lab services. They do not want to lose a potential customer for life over a small amount of free lab services. If they do not agree to compensate you, then you have two choices; get angry and sour your relationship with the film lab, or bite the bullet and move forward.

You will be very nervous until the moment when you actually get to see your footage. Sometimes a film lab will not have a screening appointment available for several weeks, so you should call them and make an appointment as soon as possible. It is a good idea to call the lab's scheduling department the same day you drop off your film.

Be prepared for your screening appointment

When your appointment day finally comes, you need to show up early. You need to bring all of your DAT tapes and log sheets with you, and hand them over to the projection room technician before your session begins so you can have sound when you watch your "dailies" up on the screen. Some labs require that you give these items to the technician at least one day before your appointment date in order to have everything ready when you walk in.

Take plenty of notes during your screenings

As you are watching your dailies, it is a good idea to take notes about anything you see that you like, or don't like. Write down notes about such things as your favorite takes of each shot, any footage that has technical deficiencies, or any scenes that must be deleted from the film. The notes that you write down during the screening process will help to save you time later when you are editing.

Be prepared for the worst, and hope for the best when you are screening your dailies

When things all go your way when you first see your dailies you will be on cloud nine. If the footage turns out to be good, and the performances are right on the mark, the feeling of elation is indescribable. When all of your hard work finally starts to show some results, and the reality of being an independent filmmaker whose dream is starting to come to fruition sets in, you start to feel quite wonderful. I have had plenty of these type of daily screening sessions, but I have also had a few of the other kind. Those are the kind that will inflict unspeakable grief upon your artistic soul, and cause you to question your resolve to be a filmmaker. This is the time when your resiliency and ingenuity are tested, and the success of your film project comes into jeopardy.

Do not dwell on bad film footage; think of a solution instead, and move forward

If any of your footage turns out to be ruined because of mistakes made during the filming process, do not panic. You will just have to alter the storyline of your movie to accommodate the loss of that footage. Unfortunately, you do not have a big enough budget to do re-shoots. Hopefully, you will not have too much bad footage.

Take *all* of your film dailies and negatives home with you after the screening session

When your viewing session is over and you have seen all of your dailies, tell the projectionist that you want to take home all of your film negatives, prints, and log sheets when you leave the session. You will need these items to cut your work print, negative, etc... You will be cutting the work print yourself, but you should hire a professional negative cutting place to cut your negative.

• TITLES AND CREDITS-

Before you start editing your film, you need to have your titles and credits made. They need to be done on 16mm film so you can edit them on to the beginning and end of your film negative Master.

Keep your titles and credits simple

Titles and credits are the names you see at the beginning and end of a film that describe the jobs that were performed by the people who worked on the film. *Titles* appear at the beginning, and should include only the major players of the movie (famous stars, directors, producers, etc…). *Credits* appear at the end, and should include everyone that worked on the film.

There are many different ways to do your titles and credits, but the best way for a low budget filmmaker is the cheapest way, of course. The cheapest way is to just do the standard white lettering over a black screen. If you try to get too creative, it will end up costing you a lot of money. You cannot spend very much money on this part of your film if you want to have any left over to finish the rest of your post-production process. Unless you can find someone who will give you a really good deal to make your titles

POST-PRODUCTION   /   193.

and credits with a computer program, and then transfer them to a 16mm film negative, it is probably best that you keep them very basic. White letters over a black screen is all that is required for an independent film with a miniscule budget. Remember, your film does not need *bells and whistles* to be good.

The titles at the beginning of a film should start with the name of the studio or production company that backed the film, and then should be followed by the names of the principal actors in the film. You should highlight any names of actors that have any fame attached to them. *Your* name and title should be the last one that is seen at the beginning of the movie. It should be displayed prominently, and held on the screen for at least five seconds.

Credits should begin with *your* name and job functions displayed on the screen prominently. Then, it should be followed by the standard *credit crawl* (slowly scrolling text) with the names of your principal actors. After that you should have the most important members of your crew (DP/Cinematographer/Grip, AD/Production Manager/Grip, Script Supervisor/PA/Grip, etc...). You, as the Producer/Director/(Writer) of the film should have your credit displayed most prominently of all. Your name (and job functions) should be the first one seen when the credits come up at the end of the movie.

Make sure you include the name of every person who worked on your film in your credits. Even the people who only worked a little bit on your film, and were not significant players, you should put their names and job functions in the credits at the end of the film.

POST-PRODUCTION / 194.

As for the principal people from your cast and crew who have it written into their contracts that they will receive a "film title and credit" as part of their payment agreement, they should have a *title* displayed prominently at the beginning of the movie, and a top *credit* at the end.

The best way to find a person/place to do your titles is to ask the people at your film lab if they can refer you to someone. They work with many independent filmmakers on a daily basis, and they are sure to know a few people/places that do titles and credits for these types of clients.

You can also find people/places that do titles and credits for independent filmmakers by going to any of the websites below.

- http://www.filmstaff.com/index.asp?camp=1

- http://www.mandy.com/

- http://www.la411.com/

- http://www.ny411.com/

All you have to do is visit these websites and click on any post-production section, then enter "titles and credits" in the search box. You should have plenty of choices to choose from.

- **EDITING-**

POST-PRODUCTION   /   195.

After you have seen your footage, it is time to start editing your movie. You will be doing most of the editing of your film yourself. It would be nice to hire a professional editor to edit your entire film, but your small budget will not permit this to happen.

There are several different methods of editing a film. Some filmmakers like to transfer their film footage *straight* to videotape or a digital format and do their editing electronically. This method allows them to make substantial corrections to color and exposure. It also allows them to add a lot of CGI (computer generated image) special effects. The final product is a Master that is on a videotape, DVD, or CD, instead of being on 16mm film. Editing your Master on a tape or digital source is only good if you plan to go *straight* to television with your film, or if you already have a *good* distribution deal lined up.

As I stated earlier; in order to be a major player at any film festivals, you must have your movie available to be projected on "the big screen", and that requires that you have a 16mm film print. Since film festivals are the best way to make a name for your movie and get a distribution deal, I strongly suggest that you edit your master on film. Most festivals will accept your movie on videotape, DVD, or CD, but it will not be screened to the festival audiences on the big screen if it wins any awards. They do have video screenings at most film festivals, but most people go to film festivals to see their movies up on the big screen. There is not much chance of your movie creating a *buzz* at any film festivals if nobody sees it. If you want your movie to have a chance to get a good distribution deal, or possibly even

POST-PRODUCTION   /   196.

hit it big, you must make it available to be screened on 16mm film.

Use a *Moviola* to edit your film

The best way, as well as the cheapest way to edit a film when you are working with a very tight budget, and you are ultimately planning to enter it in film contests, is to use the good old-fashioned 16mm *Moviola*. The Moviola is a viewing/editing machine that has been used since the 1920s by filmmakers around the world to edit their movies. These machines come in 35mm and 16mm "upright" or "flatbed" models. The 35mm models are very expensive (as with anything that has to do with 35mm film), but the 16mm models are quite cheap. These good prices are due to the fact that most people who shoot on 16mm transfer straight to a video or digital source to edit their Master, and therefore have no need for the Moviola.

You can buy a used Moviola for about $500-1500, depending on the condition of the machine. There are various people and places that sell Moviolas on the internet (just do a search with the keyword "Moviola"). You can also rent one for about $15/day, or $50/week from places that rent out film editing equipment. To find these places, just do a keyword search with the words "Moviola rentals", or do a search on any of the film production web sites that I have listed throughout this book.

You must transfer your sound first

Before you begin editing with the Moviola, you need to have your DAT tapes transferred to 16mm *full coat* sound.

POST-PRODUCTION   /   197.

Most film labs can have this done for you at their facility. If not, then they will give you information about film industry sound places that do this kind of work. The 16mm sound reels that you get from them will be used to sync up the sound and picture of your film when you are working with the Moviola.

   When you use a Moviola to edit your film, you will literally be putting your film together by hand. You will start by viewing the prints that you brought home from the film lab, and then you will choose the best pieces of footage.

   Next, you will cut up your prints and your full coat footage and take out all of your chosen pieces. As you are doing this you will number and label each one carefully with a grease pencil, and then hang them over your *film bin*. A *film bin* is basically a large, canvas laundry basket that has hooks attached to a pipe frame that hangs over the bin. You can hang each piece of film you cut on one of the hooks and let the film hang down into the basket. The purpose of using a *film bin* is to organize your pieces of film, and have them easily accessible when you are putting together your work print.

   After you have cut up your film and labeled everything clearly you will need to use splicing tape to tape all of your shots together. You will take this footage that you have just cut up and put it on 16mm film reels. This is the part where you put your movie together one shot at a time. This will be your *work print*. You will use your storyboard as a rough blueprint to work with during the editing process. It is unlikely that your final edit will be *exactly* like your

POST-PRODUCTION   /   198.

storyboard, due to changes that you were forced to make during the production process. You will also make an audio track with the 16mm *full coat* footage, and use it as a reference to sync up your sound.

You must be diligent with writing down your *edge-code numbers*

As you are splicing your shots together, you must make a log sheet that includes the beginning and end of the *edge-code numbers* for each shot. These numbers are on the edge of your film. You will also make a log sheet for your *full coat* audio track. Your work print and log sheets are essentially the blueprint for the structure of your film. The negative cutter that you eventually hire will use these numbers to cut your film negative Master.

Educate yourself on editing with a *Moviola* before you edit your film

If you have never edited a film with a Moviola, do not worry, for you can learn how to do it very easily just by reading a book. There have been plenty of books published over the years about how to use the Moviola to edit films. All you have to do is go to EBay, Amazon.com, or any similar website and enter "Moviola" in the search box. You will find plenty of books to choose from that give detailed instructions on how to edit with a Moviola. You can purchase one of these books on the internet, or just go to your favorite book store and buy one there.

There are some general rules you should keep in mind when you are editing your film.

POST-PRODUCTION   /   199.

Rule #1- Make sure the pacing of your film is relatively fast. Dramatic scenes usually require a slower pace than action scenes, but you should not make them too slow. You should not make any shot longer than you *have* to. Remember, you want to end up with a total running time of about 80-90 minutes. The main reason for this is to cut down on the cost of having film prints made, as well as all the other costs that are associated with the final process of making your film.

Another reason it is a good idea to make the pacing of your movie generally fast is to keep your audiences interested. Most people do not have the patience that is required to sit through a slow-paced film. Of course, there are some scenes that cannot be hurried, like a dramatic dying scene, or any scene that requires the audience to make an emotional investment. Just try not to have too many of those types of scenes. These scenes should be sprinkled in with your fast paced scenes that make up the majority of your film.

Rule #2- Do not use any footage that is out of focus, over/under exposed, scratched, or damaged in any way. Even if a piece of bad film is the only footage you have of a particular shot, and you feel that it is a very important part of the film, you still should not use it if it looks bad. You must have a high standard when it comes to deciding what footage to use in your film. You should only use your best footage, or you run the risk of having too low of a production value, even for cable television.

Rule #3- Make sure you match the *look* for every shot within a scene. For example; you should not cut to a close up that has a much different exposure than the other shots in that scene. When your shots do not match, your film not only looks unprofessional, but it tends to look unnatural to the viewer. If there are too many shots in your film that do not match, it could lead to an erosion of your viewer's suspension of disbelief. If this happens, they will lose interest in your film. You can adjust the exposure of a shot 1-2 f-stops when you do your "timing" later on during the final process of creating your film negative Master. This will help you a little bit to match your shots, but not very much. It is *your* responsibility to choose matching shots by how they look when you run them through the Moviola.

Rule #4- Do not break the *180 degree rule*. This is the basic editing rule that says your camera shots for any scene should all stay within an imaginary 180 degree arc that surrounds the scene. For example; you cannot have a three-shot that shows everyone in the scene with a profile, looking to their *right*, then cut to a close-up of one person that was shot from an angle on the complete opposite side of the three-shot angle, and shows that person in profile looking to their *left*. It is very important that you follow this rule to maintain a sense of realism within your scenes. When you break the 180 degree rule, it can have a jarring effect on the audience, and it can make the scene appear to look unrealistic.

Rule #5- Be diligent when it comes to continuity. Make sure there are no aspects of your scenes that do not match. Whether it is the props in a scene, the costumes, the hair styles of the characters, the positioning of the furniture, the lighting, or any other aspect, they must all be the same in each shot within a scene. Once again, if you bring inconsistencies to the attention of your audience, they will no longer suspend their disbelief, and they will dismiss your film as being amateurish. If your Script Supervisor/PA/Grip did their job well during the filming process, you should not have too much of a problem with continuity during the editing process. Among their other responsibilities this person is also in charge of keeping everything in place on the set when you are filming.

Educate yourself about film editing

If you are not very knowledgeable on the subject of film editing, then I suggest that you read up on this topic before you begin the process. You can find plenty of books on how to edit films if you go to EBay or Amazon.com (or any similar website) and enter the words "film editing" in the search box. You can also find many books on this topic at any major book store.

- **CUTTING YOUR NEGATIVE-**

After you have finished cutting your work print, it is time to cut your film negative. It is possible to cut your negative yourself, but it is not a good idea. This is far too sensitive of a process, with way too much at stake to risk doing it yourself. You only have one original film negative for each roll of your film that you shot, and you cannot take back any mistakes you might make in the cutting room. You are much more likely to have fingerprints, scratches, or dirt on your negative if you cut it yourself.

You should hire a professional to cut your negative

POST-PRODUCTION   /   202.

Some filmmakers like to make a duplicate negative from their originals to be used as backups, in case the originals are damaged, but you do not have this luxury when you are working with a very, very, low budget. That is why you need to hire a professional negative cutter to cut your film negative. A person who cuts film negatives for a living is much less likely than you are to make mistakes when it comes to cutting your negative.

It is not a good idea to bring your negative to a person/place that does not have a lot of experience. Even if a person/place is a lot cheaper than anyone else you talked to, it is not a good enough reason to trust them with your precious film negative. You may think that you are saving money, but if they damage your negative, the final product of your film production can be compromised, or even ruined.

The best way to find a person/place that you can trust to cut your negative is to ask the people at the film lab where you brought your film for processing, prints, etc... The people who work at film labs know all the best negative cutting people/places in town, and they are usually happy to give you any information regarding this matter.

Another way you can find people/places that cut film negatives is to visit any of the following film industry related websites:

- http://www.filmstaff.com/index.asp?camp=1

- http://www.mandy.com/

POST-PRODUCTION / 203.

- http://www.la411.com/

- http://www.ny411.com/

To find information about negative cutting people/places on these websites, just click on any *post-production* section, and enter the words "negative cutters" in the search boxes.

Once you have decided on a person/place to cut your negative, you should try to work out a deal with them on the price. Most reputable negative cutting people/places have a standard rate for their services, but it will not hurt to ask for a deal any way. Tell them about your budget constraints, as well as your plans to enter your film in all the major film festivals. They may give you a discount if you offer to give them a prominent film credit at the end of your film.

• MAKING A "WINDOW COPY" TRANSFER-

After your film negative Master has been edited together, you need to bring it to a place that does 16mm film transfers to video with a *telecine* machine. If the film lab that you have been using does telecine film transferring, it is a good idea to use them also for this step. Most good film labs will be able to offer you this service. If they do not, then you must find a reputable place that does 16mm film transfers to video with a *telecine* machine. Once again, just ask the people at the film lab, and they should be able to refer you to some good places that offer this type of service.

When you schedule your appointment to transfer your film to video, you need to tell the person you speak with that you will be transferring your film *with* sound, and that you will *not* need any "scene to scene" color or exposure corrections. Tell them all you want is a "one pass" transfer that is done as quickly as possible, with no stops for color or exposure corrections.

The hourly rate for telecine transfers can be quite expensive, so you want to get this first transfer done as fast as you can. You will worry about all the exposure and color details later on when you do your final transfer, after your film is complete.

You are only doing this first film transfer so you can give your Sound Designer/Mixer person a "window copy" to work with when they design and mix the sound for your film. All they need is an image to work with, and it does not have to be pretty. A window copy is basically a rough transfer that has a little window "burned" into the picture that shows time code. Your Sound Designer/Mixer will use this time code to sync up the visuals of your film with the audio.

Before you schedule this first film transfer appointment, you need to ask your Sound Designer/Mixer what format they need you to transfer your film to, in order to make sure it is compatible with whatever equipment they have in their studio. *Beta-SP* or *DigiBeta* are the most commonly used formats for independent filmmakers who transfer their films.

• SOUND DESIGN AND MIXING-

Besides a good story, your film must also have good sound. Whether it is a person at a film festival, or someone at home watching your movie on cable television, people do not like movies with bad sound quality. You can have shots that are a little over-exposed, slightly grainy, or even a bit out of focus (in the name of artistic license), but you cannot have sound that is unpleasing to the human ear. Your sound quality must be crisp, clear, and as good as any other movie that is winning on the film festival circuit today, or people will discredit your film for being unprofessional, and then they will move on to the next one.

After you have made your *window copy* transfer, it is time to put together the *final mix* of the sound for your movie. You can do it yourself, or you can hire a professional to do it for you.

The best way to pay your post-production sound people is to give them 40% of the money up front and 60% when you receive the CD or DAT tape of your *final mix*. Make sure you draw up a release form specifically for them, and have them sign it before you give them their down payment.

Hiring people to do post-production sound work used to cost a lot of money. There were relatively few professionals doing this kind of work, mostly due to the fact that it just cost too much money to buy the equipment that was needed to perform this task.

Nowadays, a person can pay $500 for a computer program and get the capability to do professional quality sound designing, recording, and mixing on their home computer. Computer software programs like *Cubase* and *Pro Tools* have revolutionized the state of the professional sound industry. Sound work that could only be done in an expensive sound studio in Hollywood before is now being done in the homes of people who live all over the world. Sound technology has advanced greatly in the last decade, and this has made it much easier for independent filmmakers to get professional sound work at a relatively low price.

If you do not want to spend the time and the money to buy one of these programs and learn how to use it, then you can hire a Sound Designer/Mixer to do it for you at a reasonable rate. There are a lot more people doing this type of work these days than ever before, and they are always looking for work. This is a good thing for independent filmmakers, for they can now have good quality sound on their films without having to spend an arm and a leg to get it.

Before you do the sound designing and mixing for your film, you must hire someone to create the music. The musical score of a film is a very important element, so you should not take it lightly. The right music can enhance the moods of your scenes, and touch emotional buttons with your audience. The wrong music can annoy your audience, and even drive them out of the theater.

There are a lot of talented musicians out there that do music for independent films at a reasonable price.

Unfortunately for them, there are not a lot of high paying jobs available in this field. The people who are not famous yet are forced to earn their living working on smaller films, and that is where you can benefit. All you have to do is look for these people, request CDs of their work, and choose a person who is very talented, but has not yet had their "big break". You can usually find someone to do your music for only a few thousand dollars, as long as you offer them a prominent film credit at the beginning, and the end of the film.

Find someone who is multi-talented to do the sound for your movie

Some Sound Designers/Mixers who work on independent films are also talented musicians who can do the music for your film along with the designing and mixing parts. Finding someone who is a jack-of-all-trades with post-production sound work is the best idea, for you will usually get a package deal. Just make sure that the person you hire has just as much musical talent as they do technical talent, or your film will be severely compromised.

Keep it simple with your sound

The post-production sound work for a film with a miniscule budget should be very basic. It should consist of syncing up dialogue, adding music, and laying down a few sound effects where needed. Overall, your sound work should be uncomplicated, yet very professional sounding. You will not be adding very much in the way of special sound effects or complicated mixes. It is the same here as it is with all the other aspects of your film; the idea is to get

POST-PRODUCTION / 208.

the job done as quickly and as cheaply as possible, yet with good quality work.

The best way to find good, affordable people who do post-production sound work for independent films is to ask the people behind the desk at the sound equipment rental houses in your area. They can usually refer you to several people who do this kind of work. You can also ask the Soundman (person) that you hired to record your sound if they know anyone. Whether it is designing, recording, or mixing sound, these people all work in the same field, and they can usually supply you with names and numbers of people that do all different aspects of sound for independent filmmakers.

You can also find people/places that do music and/or sound design/mixing for independent films by searching for them on the internet.

Websites that offer information about people and places that do music, sound design/mixing, etc… for independent films:

- http://www.filmstaff.com/index.asp?camp=1

- http://www.mandy.com/

- http://www.la411.com/

- http://www.ny411.com/

To find information about people/places that do sound design and/or mixing for independent films you can visit these websites, and click on any *post-production* section. Then, just enter the words "sound designers and mixers". To find people who do music for movies enter "film scoring" or "music for films" in the search boxes.

If you do hire someone to do your music and/or sound designing and mixing it is a good idea to work very closely with them when they work on your film. Do not just give them a list of the things you need from them, and then tell them to call you when they have completed the *final mix*. You should keep in touch with them on every step of this process. Tell them that you want to be part of every aspect of the work they do for you, and that they can feel free to call you on your cell phone anytime they have any questions about your film. You must make sure every aspect of the sound work they give you is professional quality work, and that everything is being done according to your specifications. For example, if the music is too loud for a certain scene, you need to tell them to bring down the level a little on that particular *track* before they do the *final mix*. If a piece of music does not capture the mood that you are looking for, then you must tell the person who composed it that they need to do it again until they get it right. Stress to them the importance of this matter, but do not insult them in any way.

Work hard, but have fun too

Doing the post-production sound for your film is hard work, but it can also be very fun as well. Creating *foley* effects is the highlight of the post-production sound experience. *Foley* is the film industry word that people use to explain the process of creating sound effects in a studio or on a sound stage. Extraordinary methods are often employed to create sounds effects for such things that range from every day noises, to sounds you have never heard before.

It can be very challenging to create ordinary sounds using extraordinary methods. For example; I once worked with a sound designer/mixer to create the sound of a rope stretching. We did it by twisting the sleeve of a leather jacket as I held it up to a microphone. It sounded exactly like a rope stretching. Another time we created the sound of a landslide by rolling a box of dirt and rocks down a cardboard ramp. The results were great, and we had a lot of fun achieving them.

While it is true that creating *foley* sound effects can be fun to do, they can also be very time consuming, and that means expensive. When it comes to any work that is done on your film, time is money (as you are well aware of by this point), so you should only use *foley* effects where you absolutely need them. You should always try to use a "canned" sound effect from a sound effects library CD first, before you decide that a *foley* effect is necessary. Any good sound designer/mixer that works on independent films usually has an extensive CD sound effects library that includes almost every sound effect you can think of in the world, and some from out of this world. It is a lot quicker and cheaper to lay down something from a CD than it is to create a whole new sound.

The final product that you need to get from your sound designer/mixer is a CD or DAT tape of your *final mix*. This mix will have your dialogue, music, and sound effects on it.

POST-PRODUCTION / 211.

It must all be mixed very professionally, with all the correct levels that you specified on each *track* for every scene. This CD or DAT tape must also have a "two-pop" at the beginning (two beeping sounds) so the lab technician can have a reference point to sync up the sound when you get your prints made.

• MAKING PRINTS OF YOUR MOVIE-

Making prints of your movie is the last step of the post-production process. You will be having this done at the same film lab that you brought your film to for processing, screening, etc... You will need to provide them with your *film negative Master,* and the CD or DAT tape of your audio *final mix.* Tell the scheduler that you want a *16mm film print(s)* with an *optical track (*sound*).* An *optical track* is a sound track of your final mix that is laid down near the edge of the film print. A special optical sound head on the industry standard film projectors picks up the sound when your film runs through it.

You must also tell the scheduler at the film lab that you want an *aspect ratio* of 1:85 for your film print(s). This determines the dimensions of your images on the screen. 1:85 is your standard rectangular screen image, like all the movies you see in the theaters.

It is a wonderful moment when you are finally holding that 16mm film print in your hand, and you know that your film is officially completed, and ready for the world to see.

• TRANSFERRING YOUR FILM TO VIDEO/DVD -

Before you start filling out those film festival entry forms, you need to have your film transferred to videotape or DVD. This will be done on a *telecine* machine. When you are done you will have your *videotape or DVD Master*. This is the Master that you will use to make all of your other copies from, including any VHS or DVD copies you will need to send out to film festivals with your entry forms.

Try to use the same lab for all your post-production film and video services

Most film labs also offer transfer services in addition to their other film services. It is a good idea to use the same lab that you have been using throughout your film production process. You have already established a relationship with them, and you do not want to trust your film negative Master and your audio CD or DAT tape Master with someone you have not worked with in the past.

If your film lab does not do film to tape transfers, then you can find plenty of places that do this kind of work by just doing a *keyword* search on the internet using the words "16mm film to tape transfers". You will have plenty of places to choose form, but I suggest that you choose one very carefully.

Cheaper film-to-tape transfer services does not necessarily mean better

The cost for film-to-tape transfers varies from about $100/hour to $350/hour. Be leery of places that offer the lowest price in town, for you usually get what you pay for with this kind of work.

To transfer your film to videotape you must schedule an appointment with the place you choose. Tell the scheduler that you want to do a *"scene-to-scene* supervised transfer", which basically means that you want to be there when the transfer is happening so you can give directions regarding color and exposure corrections. This will make the transfer process go a bit slower, which will cost you a little more money than a "*one-pass*" transfer, but it is worth it to be able to correct a few of your color and exposure deficiencies. Remember, distributors, as well as the people who decide whether or not your film gets accepted in film festivals will make their decisions based on what they see on the VHS or DVD copy you send them, so you want it to look as good as possible.

You must tell the scheduler what format you plan to use when you are making your a film-to-tape transfer appointment, so they can provide the transfer technician with a new tape before your transfer session begins. Most places will not allow you to bring your own blank tape, for fear that it might not be up to their standards, and could damage their expensive equipment if it is dirty, or even worse, breaks during the transfer process.

Beta-SP and *DigiBeta* are the most commonly used formats by independent filmmakers for their *videotape Masters*.

POST-PRODUCTION   /   214.

To transfer your film to videotape, you need to take your 16mm film negative Master and your CD or DAT tape audio Master to the facility of your choosing. When you are doing the transfer, it is important to remember that you are paying hundreds of dollars per hour for this process, and you want to finish it as soon as possible. You do not need to do a color or exposure correction for every shot. You should only stop down to make corrections at places in your film where you absolutely need it.

After your transfer to videotape is complete, it is now time to share your film vision with the public. It is time to get your film sent out to film festivals. Hopefully, your film will be accepted in one of the major film festivals like *Sundance* or *Toronto,* the public will like your movie, and it will lead to a film distribution deal.

9

Distribution

The best place to start on your quest to secure a distribution deal for your film is the film festival circuit. The idea is to create a *buzz* about your movie by word of mouth, until it takes on a life of it's own. If it is a positive *buzz*, the distribution agents will come running to you with offers in hand, and believe me, these offers will be much better than the ones you would typically get from them if your film never had that *buzz* created about it.

When you are a filmmaker working with a small budget you cannot afford to spend money to advertise your film. The best (and cheapest) way for you to find audiences to see your movie is to have it shown at film festivals. If your film is well liked, the festivals will do all the advertising for you, and it won't cost you a penny. Most film festivals only charge about $50 for their entry fees. All you have to do to enter a film festival is obtain an entry form from the contest officials (most can be downloaded from festival websites), fill it out, and then send it in before the deadline. You must also send a check or money order for the entry fee costs and a videotape or DVD of your movie. It is also a good idea to send a few promotional still photos and a small press package that explains what your movie is about, where it was filmed, who is starring in it, etc… You can make this package yourself on your home computer with a graphics

DISTRIBUTION   /   216.

program like *Adobe Photoshop,* or even *Microsoft Word.* Do an internet search for *press packages,* and you will find plenty of results that you can model your package around.

Your tape will be screened by a panel of film festival judges. If they like it, they will ask you to send them a 35mm or 16mm film print. They will use this print to show your movie on the "big screen" to the people who attend their film festival. When the festival is over they will send your print back and you can use it for other film festivals.

Every movie that is accepted into one of the prestigious film festivals has the potential to make it big

There have been some incredible success stories about small movies that made it big on the film festival circuit. (*El Mariachi, The Blair Witch Project, etc...*). If your movie does extremely well at a major film festival like *The Sundance Film Festival,* or *Cannes,* then you will get a good distribution deal, and your film may end up showing in theaters nationwide! Whoever buys your film may invest money to have the production value improved and blown up to 35mm. They may also want to sell your movie on videotape and DVD. All of this would be great if it happens, but it is more likely that you will get a small distribution deal, and you will *not* be on all the evening news shows across the country. It is a very rare occasion when a small movie makes it to the mainstream media spotlight, but it does happen once in a while.

Having your movie shown in theaters nationwide should be your dream, but cable television should be your goal

Most small movies that secure distribution deals at film festivals are destined to end up on cable television. Movies that show on cable do not always need to have an expensive looking production value. The movie that you make for $50,000 could end up playing on cable television channels all over the world, as long as it has the minimum requirements for production value. You could even make a decent profit.

The best film festivals to enter are the ones that get the most media attention, like *The Sundance Film Festival, The Toronto Film Festival, Cannes, The Santa Barbara Film Festival,* etc... Of course these are the hardest ones to get accepted into, so you better be very confident that your movie is unique and very well made before you decide to enter it, or you will just waste your time and money. On top of that, you will only end up being disappointed. You must be realistic about how good or bad you film really is before you enter any contests.

All you need is a little media attention

All the major media outfits send crews and reporters to the highest profile film festivals. They usually spend a whole week reporting on things like the celebrities that happen to show up, the circus-like atmospheres, and most importantly, any movies that have created a *buzz*. If your movie gets any kind of media attention, the monetary value increases quite dramatically. If your movie gets *a lot* of media attention, it will most definitely lead to a very profitable distribution deal, and it may even lead to work on bigger and better film projects.

There is still room for the small filmmakers at the big film festivals

While these big-name film festivals were originally created to give attention to unknown independent filmmakers, they have for the most part been taken over by the high profile Hollywood movie scene these days. Celebrities and big Hollywood *players* are attracted to these festivals for a variety of reasons, but the main reason is simply because the media spotlight is there to give them publicity. Despite this fact, most of the major film festivals still make room for some of the smaller movies to share the spotlight with the bigger ones. All you need is a little piece of their spotlight to catch the attention of the film distribution sales agents who frequent these festivals.

If your film does not get accepted into any of the big-name film festivals, then you should go ahead and send it to some of the smaller film festivals. Film distribution sales agents also attend these festivals to look for movies that are hidden gems, or even ones that are not so great. As I mentioned in previous pages, there is a big demand for independent films to fill the programming schedules of literally thousands of broadcast and cable channels around the world.

The best way to find information about the numerous film festivals out there is to do a *keyword* search on the internet with the words "film festivals", or "film contests". You will get information about all kinds of film festivals, big and small.

Your film does not need to have a spectacular production value to secure a distribution deal. As long as you adhere to the minimum requirements that I have laid out in this book in terms of visuals and audio, and you have a good story, your movie can do very well at film festivals. If this happens, you will almost certainly get a distribution deal. If you do secure a distribution deal at one of these festivals, your movie will probably end up being seen mostly on cable television. The production value standards of some cable TV channels are much lower than those of the broadcast channels, and a film like yours could be just what they are looking for to fill their twenty-four hour a day programming schedules.

There are a lot of distribution agents who go to film festivals to make distribution deals with undiscovered filmmakers. If your film does well you should not have very much trouble finding one of these agents. Trust me, they will find you if there is a *buzz* created about your film.

If you do not want to try your luck on the film festival circuit, then you can go straight to the distributors yourself. There are film and television content markets like NATPE and MIPCOM, but getting a booth setup at these conventions to display your product can cost thousands of dollars. You can also find a list of distribution companies on the internet. The problem with these methods is that you really have no leverage to bargain with, because your movie has never received any critical acclaim anywhere. Critical acclaim with the public and the media is your best bargaining chip when you are trying to make a distribution deal. It shows that your film has value. Without it, your film will get no respect from the distributors.

Websites that offer information about film distribution companies:

- http://www.aems.uiuc.edu/HTML/distributors.las

- http://sunsite.berkeley.edu/cgi-bin/db_mrc.pl?type=Distributor

- http://www.business.com/directory/media_and_entertainment/film/distributors/

- http://www.indievisionfilms.homestead.com/

Most film distribution companies will give you a ridiculously low offer when you call them to make a deal. They are hardened business people who see hundreds of independent films each year, and they know how to get good deals for their companies.

Do not accept the first offer that you get from a distribution company. You need to shop your film around to many different companies. Your movie may be worth more to one company than it is to another, so make sure you send a videotape or DVD copy out to many different places. Be sure to indicate somewhere on the videotape or DVD that it is a "screener" copy, and that you hold all the rights to your film.

You must try to drive a hard bargain with the distribution companies that you deal with, or all of your hard work on your film will give you very little payoff.

DISTRIBUTION   /   221.

If you get a distribution deal for your film, you *are* officially a *professional* filmmaker. It does not matter how much money you make, as long as you make a profit. Once you realize that you have fulfilled your dream to make a movie and sell it, you will only be inspired even more to make another one. The more films you make, the more your profits will increase, for you will only learn more each time about how the business works.

Some people have greater success than others in the film industry. Whether your film makes it to the national media spotlight, or finds a home on some obscure cable channel, the important thing to remember is that you had a dream, and you followed it. There is nothing more fulfilling than knowing that you accomplished a life-long goal.

I wish you luck with your goal to make movies, and I hope that this book provided you with some insight and knowledge that will benefit you in the pursuit of your dream to be a filmmaker.

Keep your dreams alive and never let your creative vision fade.

Michael P. Connelly

www.makealowbudgetmovie.com

Copyright 2005.   Michael P. Connelly

ISBN 0-9770500-0-9

Glossary of Film Industry Terms

• • • •

action: 1. The word that film directors yell out on a movie set when they want their actors to begin acting in a scene. **2.** A word that describes any part of a movie that is fast paced or exiting. **3.** A sequence of plot developing events that is related to the characters in the movie, and helps to move the story to a dramatic conclusion.

act one, two, and three: The classic dramatic structure of a story that contains a beginning (act one), middle (act two), and end (act three).

adaptation: The transforming of a story from one medium to another medium. This process is most commonly associated with taking a best-selling novel and turning it into a motion picture.

agent: A person that is paid on commission to broker a deal between creative talent and the production companies in the film industry.

angle: 1. The point of view of a movie that can determine whether or not it is ground breaking, different, interesting, unusual, etc... **2.** Any image that the cinematographer sees when they are looking through the camera lens. This is determined by the location and positioning of a film camera.

antagonist: The primary character or element in a story that opposes the antagonist (main character). This can be a person, a force of nature, an organization, government, etc...

attachment: Film industry term that refers to any bankable talent and management people that have signed on to a film (movie stars, famous directors, producers, etc...). This is a very important factor in the decision-making process of getting funding and backing for a motion picture.

based on a true story: A term that refers to a film that is about an actual event or story that occurred in the past. It must contain a minimal amount of fictionalization and embellishment.

bidding war: A battle that ensues when two or more buyers are interested in buying a motion picture script. This war is usually conducted between the agents and managers of the interested buyers and the scriptwriter.

buzz: A film industry term that is associated with word of mouth publicity about a film. This is usually a positive thing for any film, but if it is an unusually bad one, it can have a negative buzz surrounding it.

cable: A type of television service that is delivered via cable for a monthly fee.

canned: A word that refers to any creative effects that are taken from a pre-recorded source instead of being created from scratch.

characters: All of the individuals who play a part in a story. A character can be living, dead, real, or fictional, but as long as they are referred to in the script as a person who is part of the storyline, then they are considered a character.

chemistry: A term that refers to the idea that some artists work very well together, and some do not. Having chemistry between artists on a movie set can be the deciding factor in the success or failure of a film. If there is no chemistry, the film usually fails.

cliffhanger: Any film that offers genuine suspense that keeps the audience members on the edges of their seats and eager to see what happens next.

close-up (CU): A camera angle that features a single person and is framed from the shoulders up.

collaboration: A bonding of creative efforts that usually refers to the major players of a film production (producers, directors, stars, etc…).

comedy: 1. Any film that is about a humorous subject, and not a drama in any way. **2.** The act of performing a humorous scene.

comp, or complimentary: A term that refers to anything that a film studio or production company provides at no charge to the people who work for them (cast, crew, management, promotional people, etc...) during the process of making and selling a film.

conflict: The state of disharmony, or opposition that exists between characters in a dramatic story. This is a very important factor in driving the storyline along, and keeping the audience interested.

co-producer: A film production position that is just below producer. This job description involves helping the producers of the film do anything that must be done to make a film production go smoothly.

copyright: The right that an individual holds for any creative work. This right is protected by federal law as declared by the U.S. Copyright Office of the Library of Congress.

creative elements: A term that refers to the major elements that are "attached" to a film project (directors, stars, famous writers, etc...).

crawl: A term that is most often used during the post-production phase to describe lettering or graphics that are superimposed over the screen, and then move slowly up, down, or across the screen. This term describes what happens when the "credits roll" at the end of a movie.

credits: A term that refers to the list of people you see at the end of a film along with the functions they performed during the process of making the film. This term is not to be confused with the term *titles,* which appear at the beginning of a film, and include only the major *players* in the film.

CUT: 1. The word that a film director yells out on a movie set when they want filming to stop immediately. This is the official signal that tells everyone on the set to stop what they are doing. **2.** An immediate change from one shot to another shot on the screen.

CUT TO: A term that refers to the immediate transition of one scene to another scene on the screen. This direction is always capitalized when it is written in the script.

demographic: The study of a particular audience and the statistics that define their tastes in movies. This is the most important word associated with whether or not a major film studio decides to invest in a particular type of movie. They do a lot of research before they invest in a movie to make sure that the subject matter of the film matches the demographics of their target audience.

development: The first phase of a film project that begins when a studio or production company purchases a script, and ends with the start of the production phase. This is the period where every aspect of the film production is finalized, and includes such tasks as deciding on a cast, and choosing who will direct the film.

dialogue: 1. Any speech by the characters in a film.
2. A conversation between two people.

dissolve: The transition of one scene or shot to another one as one shot fades away, and a new one fades onto the screen.

documentary: Any film that is about an actual event and does not use actors or a script.

double: A person that fills in for an actor during any parts of the filming process where an actor or actress is not capable of performing (dangerous stunts, nude scenes, etc…).

drama: 1. Any film that is about a serious subject, and not a comedy in any way. **2.** The act of performing a serious scene.

executive producer: A title given to any person who contributes significantly to the deal making and development parts of a film, and not so much in the actual production part.

extra: Any actor in a movie that does not play a significant role. These are the people who help to create the background atmosphere in a scene.

FADE IN: The smooth transition from absolute black to showing a scene on the screen. This direction is always in capital letters in the script.

FADE OUT: The smooth transition from showing a scene on the screen to showing absolute black. This direction is always in capital letters in the script.

feature film: Any movie that is made to be shown in the major motion picture theaters.

film: 1. Any movie or motion picture. **2.** The material that is used in a motion picture camera to make a movie. **3.** The act of filming a movie.

financier: The person or company that provides the funding to make a movie.

gaffer: A lighting electrician who works on a movie set.

gaffer's tape: A roll of black multi-purpose tape that a gaffer uses on a movie set.

green light: A film industry term that describes the point when a movie has been given the okay to move forward with production.

hook: Any interesting or unique element in a film that captures the attention of the audience.

independent film: 1. Any film that is made outside of the traditional Hollywood studio system, and offers a unique perspective with original subject matter. **2.** The film industry for people who make alternative or low budget films.

independent filmmaker: Any person who makes a film outside of the traditional Hollywood studio system, and offers a unique perspective with original subject matter.

infringement: A legal term that describes a violation of the copyright act by using protected material without authorization.

interior, or INT: 1. The first part of a scene that is written in scripts to indicate that a scene will take place inside a building or structure. **2.** A word that describes any scene that will be shot indoors.

location: 1. Any place where a motion picture is filmed. A movie set. **2.** The part on the scene headings of scripts that comes right after INT., and indicates where scenes take place.

log line: A one line description of a movie that sums it up in a single sentence, with the intention of getting people to be interested in the movie.

log sheet: Any piece of paper that contains technical information related to the production of your film. The data on these sheets is written down by camera and sound people during filming, and used later on during the post-production phase for such things as syncing up sound, editing film, etc…

make-up: 1. The cosmetics that are applied to the faces of actors (lipstick, eyeliner, powders, etc…). **2.** The person or place on a movie set that the actors must visit to have their make-up applied.

manager: Any representative who works with creative talent in the film industry on all aspects of their career (marketing, promotions, health, etc...), with the overall goal in mind of advancing the careers of these clients. The main difference between a manager and an agent is that a manager cannot secure employment for their clients.

medium shot (MS): A camera angle that features a single person and is framed from the waist up

montage: 1. A quick sequence of scenes or shots in a movie with a common theme or message. **2.** A part of the scene heading that can be added to indicate a rapid sequence of shots.

motion picture: 1. A sequence of filmed images that is projected on a screen in a rapid manner to create the illusion of motion. **2.** Any movie that is shot on 16mm or 35mm film.

motivation: The driving force behind the psychological makeup of the characters in a story that determines the way that they act in the film.

movie: A motion picture, or film.

narration: Off-screen commentary that is added to a film's soundtrack. This is also commonly known as voice-over.

off screen (O.S.): Any dialogue, action, or sound that occurs during a scene that can be heard, but not seen. This term is always written on the script in it's abbreviated form with parenthesis surrounding it.

original: 1. A term that describes any material that was used as the primary source from which a movie is edited from. For example; any DAT tapes that a Soundman records while working on a movie are the original sound tapes for that film. **2.** Any movie or script that is not based on an existing story or idea.

outline: A list of every scene in a movie.

package: 1. A film industry term that describes the creative and administrative elements that have agreed to work on a motion picture. **2.** A group of film industry equipment items that can be rented for the purpose of filming a movie (camera packages, DAT recorder packages, etc…).

pan: A camera shot where the camera moves slowly from left to right, or from right to left in one continuous move.

pitch: A film industry term that describes the act of orally relating an idea for a film to a prospective buyer or financier.

plagiarism: To take and use the words of another writer and use them as your own words without legal permission to do so.

player: A film industry term that describes anyone in the industry that is in a position of power.

plot: A cumulative pattern of action and events that occurs in a movie in order to establish the storyline.

point of view (POV): 1. A camera shot that shows an angle that is supposed to be looking through the eyes of a particular character. This direction is always written on the script as an acronym and capitalized. **2.** The overall angle of a movie.

post-production: The last phase in the process of making a movie where the sound and picture of the film are edited, and the film is completed.

premise: The basic idea of any story.

pre-production: The first phase in the process of making a movie that comes right after development. This is the period where everything is prepared for the production phase (location scouting, costume design, set construction, etc…

producer: The person or company that has the overall responsibility of overseeing every step in the process of making a movie. This is the person that everyone must answer to on a film project.

production: 1. The second phase in the process of making a movie where the actual filming and recording takes place. This phase follows the pre-production phase. **2.** Any film project.

protagonist: The main character in any film that drives the storyline. This person is not necessarily the "good guy" in the movie (IE; Charles Foster Kane in *Citizen Kane*).

registration: The act of registering a script or film idea with the U.S. Copyright Office or with an organization like the Writers Guild of America.

GLOSSARY OF FILM INDUSTRY TERMS   /   233.

release form: A legal document or contract that states the responsibilities, rights, and compensation of individuals that do business with each other on a film project.

resolution: 1.The last act or scene in a movie that comes after the climax, and ties up all the loose ends. 2. A cinematography term that describes the clarity of a film image.

scene: The building blocks of a motion picture. A unit of film time for the technical breakdown of a movie's structure.

screenplay: A feature film script that is written with the intention of having it made into a motion picture.

script: 1. Another name for a screenplay. 2. Any text that a screenplay contains.

setting: Any location where a scene takes place.

shooting schedule: A schedule that is made up during the pre-production phase of a film project that determines which days each scene of the movie will be filmed. All of the scenes of a movie are broken up, and then grouped together with production budget concerns in mind. Then they are assigned days to be filmed.

shot: The basic unit of measurement in the structure of a movie that is made up of a series of frames of motion picture film.

sound effects (SFX): Any special audio effects for a film that are created by a sound designer or technician.

spec: An abbreviation of the word *speculation* that refers to any screenplay that is written without a contract or deal with the hope that it can be sold for a good price.

special effects (EFX, or FX): The altering of images and sound during the post-production phase of a movie to create a product that is different from the way it was originally shot or recorded.

superimpose (SUPER): A special effect that shows one image over another one. These kinds of effects are achieved with the use of various technical processes during the post-production phase of a movie.

synopsis: A short summation of a movie that ranges from one paragraph to three pages of writing. It is a straight-to-the-point version of a film idea that highlights the strongest elements of the film.

take: 1. The specific angle or point-of-view of a movie or a character in a movie. **2.** A film industry term for the various shots of a scene that are filmed several different times each (take one, take two, take three, etc…).

theme: The general idea that determines what a story is all about.

through line: The main theme or storyline that is prevalent throughout a movie.

GLOSSARY OF FILM INDUSTRY TERMS / 235.

title page: The front page of a screenplay that includes such information as the title, the writer's name, and any contact information.

titles: The names of people that you see at the beginning of a movie along with the job function they performed to make the film. This list of names includes only the major players of the film, as opposed to the *credits* at the end that lists everyone that worked on the film.

trades: A film industry term that refers to the major entertainment magazines that cover the Hollywood film industry (*The Hollywood Reporter, Daily Variety,* etc...).

treatment: A detailed summary of a movie idea that is written out in narrative form instead of in script format. This ten to twenty page version of a film idea is intended to give potential investors a clear idea of what a story will look like if it is made into a motion picture. It is an expanded version of the *synopsis* with details added to it.

twist: An unexpected change in the storyline of a film that is completely different than what the audience expected to see.

TWO-SHOT: A camera angle that features two people and is usually framed to show each character from the waist up.

voice-over (V.O.): This is a film industry term that describes the recorded voice or voices of a character(s) that play over images in a film. This process is performed during the post-production phase.

WGA: The acronym that is used for the Writers Guild of America. This is the primary source for screenplay writers to register their scripts before they shop them around.

ZOOM: A camera technique where the camera person moves in or out of a scene from a far away shot to a closer one, or visa versa.

ZOOM IN: A camera technique where there is a change from a shot that is far away, to a shot that closer.

ZOOM LENS: A lens for a motion picture camera that is capable of zooming in and out of a shot.

ZOOM OUT: A camera technique where there is a change from a shot that is close up, to a shot that is far away.

Index

• • • •

AAA (The Auto Club), 142-144
accidents (filming), 139-140
ad-lib lines, 136, 152-153
"add-on" lines, 153
Adobe Photoshop, 216
Adobe Reader, 15,
agents, distribution, 215, 219
alter the storyline, 191
always be in command, 129
"Always Fast and Efficient", 151
Amazon.com, 201
American Cinematographer magazine, 65
American Film magazine, 65
animated short films, 16
Araki, Gregg, 23
artistic medium, 147
arc, 180 degree, 200
arguing with cast and crew, 146-147
artistic license, 205
art of story telling, the, 181
aspect ratio, 114, 211
assembling a crew, 59-81
Assistant Director/Production Manager/Grip, 76-78, 81, 94, 102, 122, 135,
audio, 162-171, 198 (also, see sound)
available light, 31

average number of work hours (filming), 96,
Avoid Negative Energy, 154-156
backlash (cast and crew), 125
*Backstage West (*magazine), 40
bad film footage, 191
Baja California, 50
bare-bones crew, 73-81
bargaining
   at garage sales and flea markets, 111-112
   with distribution companies, 219-221
   with post-production people, 186
   with potential cast members, 45-47
   with potential crew members, 45-47, 62-63
   with script writers, 36-38
bargaining tool,
   for negotiating with actors, 45
   for negotiating with distribution companies, 219
basic needs (cast and crew), 129
bells and whistles, 21, 180, 183, 193
best film festivals, 217, 218
best image quality available, 25
best pieces of footage, 197
best wilderness locations, 58
Beta-SP, 204, 213
"big break", 35, 207
big film studios, 21, 23, 150-151, 163
big-name film festivals, 216-218
Big name Stars, 21
"big screen, the", 195, 216
Birth of a Nation, 181
Bishop, California, 127
black film bag (duffle bag), 171, 175-176

Black Mountain Way, 159
Blair Witch Project, The, 16, 21, 216
blocking, 71, 85,134
"boom operator", 75, 166, 168-169
"boom" microphone, 75, 76, 168
Bridgeport, California, 159
brief bio/resume, 36
briefcase, 107-108, 136
bring in a profit, (with a film), 27
broadcast zone (cell phone), 120
"brown-bagged" (lunches), 72
budget constraints, 47
Budget Breakdown, 83-85
business cards, 67
business side of the film industry, 19
buyer beware (film stock), 114-115
Buying Film, 112-116
buying food in bulk, 125-126
buzz, 30, 33,195, 215, 217, 219
camera person, 89
 camera rental, 64
cancellations, 59, 121-123, 128
Cannes (film festival), 216
cans of film, 174-177
caravan, 118, 120, 126
Carrey, Jim, 21
cartooning, 86
caterer, 73
celebrities (at film festivals), 218
cell phone, 119-120
cell (transmitter*)*, 120
celluloid, 155, 160
CGI (computer generated image), 195

character-driven story, 36
cheaper is not better
   with film labs, 177
   with film-to-tape transfers, 212-214
choosing your locations, 99
cinematographers, 105
Cinematography, 155
cinema verite, 89
circumventing the Hollywood system, 70
Citizen Kane, 88
Clerks, 21
CLOSE-UPS and INSERTS, 154
"cold reading", 44
collective consciousness (of film audiences), 29
color timing, 84
commercialized films, 20
commit to a road trip, 96
complain, but do not threaten (with film labs), 189
complicated camera moves, 32
computer program(s), 85, 102-103, 206
"connections", 158
connect with your audience, 30
constant arguments, 59
contingency plan(s), 132, 149
continuity, 78, 200-201
controversial political topic(s), 31
copy of the script, 78
copy of your storyboard, 85
Costco, 124-126
costly nightmares, 147
costumes, 92, 108-112, 171-174
creating a storyboard, 87
creating *foley* (sound effects), 166, 209-210

creative control, 29, 38, 44, 63, 69, 166
creative input, 166
creative process, 29, 49
creative type(s), 28, 30
creative vision, 78, 151
credit crawl, 196
Credits, 192-194
crew meetings, 100-103, 131, 132, 133-135
critical acclaim, 219
Cruise, Tom, 21
"crystal sync" (sound) camera package, 74
CSUN (California State University, Northridge), 61
Cubase, 206
"Cut!", 138, 153
cutting your negative, 201-203
cutting your *work print*, 179, 197-201
dailies, 162, 179, 185, 187-192
Daily pay,
   for your actors, 46
   for your crew members, 73-81
DAT (digital audio tape), 163-165, 168-171, 174-176, 196, 210-211, 214
daunting task(s), 59, 121
dealing with people (you encounter while filming), 53, 56-58
decent profit, 22
deficiencies in the production value, 184
Deliverance, 49
demo reels, 186
detailed labeling (the importance), 161
digital revolution, the, 25
digital slate, 162
Directing (films), 144-159

INDEX / 243.

discuss a plan (to keep equipment dry), 132
Disneyland, 150
distractions, 32
Distribution (film), 22, 24, 113, 215-221
don't be discouraged, 29
download (this book/ebook), 14
DP/Cinematographer/Grip, 73-75, 78, 80, 88-89, 101, 113-114, 122-123, 139, 155-157, 159, 162, 165, 167, 174, 193
due diligence (for location scouting), 70
Eastman Kodak, 115
easy to eat (meals), 124-126
EBay, 198
edge-code numbers, 198
editing (film), 185, 192, 194-203
efficiency, 94
"El Mariachi", 23, 216
emergency room, 141
emotional scenes, 133
entertaining story, 184
entertainment industry, 22
equipment packages (camera and DAT), 64-66, 69, 89, 156-158, 165, 177
established writer, 37
ET: The Extraterrestrial, 24
expenses, 48-49
expensive director, 21
EXPOSED FILM, 174
exposure (for your movie), 16, 37
EXTERIOR (scenes), 31, 33, 36, 52, 93
extraordinary methods (sound design), 210
extras (actors), 31, 84
eye candy, 180, 184
favorite film production story, 148-150

Federal Land (filming on), 57
feedback, 30
film artist, 181
film audiences, 20, 164, 182
film bin, 197
film commissions, 52-53, 57
film festival circuit, 14, 16-17, 22, 30, 185, 195-196, 215-219
film industry, 14, 17, 20, 26, 35, 46, 62-63, 65, 182-184
filming ratio, 104, 114
film labs, 159-160, 176-179, 187-192, 196-197, 203-205, 212
film negative, 133, 201-203, 211
film permits, 52-53, 57-58
film prints, 199, 211
film production, 22, 25, 29, 70, 77-78, 85, 115, 117, 132, 156
film production books, 18,
film-to-tape transfers, 212-214
final mix (sound), 205-211
Finding a Good, Affordable Crew, 59-81
Finding Good, Affordable Actors, 39-47
find the ideal place to shoot, 49
finished product, 106
first aid kit, 140-141
First Edition, 14-15
"fix it in post", 153, 155
fly under the radar, 57-58
Focus Puller/Camera Assistant/Grip, 74-75
foley sound effects, 166, 209-210
formula for making a movie, 19
freebie, 71
"*From Dusk Til' Dawn*", 23

fulfillment of a dream, 27
full coat (16mm), 196-198
fundamentals of film production, 25
garage sales, 109-112
general content, 15
general impression (of the film business), 18
general formula (for making a movie), 19
"golden hour", 97
good script, 35
good quality sound, 164
good story (the value of), 28, 35
Griffith, D.W., 181
grip, 90
guardian of your film vision, 78
Halloween costumes, 109
hallmarks of a great director, 150
"hand-held" camera, 101, 153, 158
hand mike, 169
headphones, 167
heart and soul of any film, 59
helping to set up meals, 79
hidden costs, 169
"highlighter" pens, 92-93
hillbillies (in *Deliverance*), 49
holding reflectors, 75, 139
Hollywood *players*, 218
Hollywood system, the, 70
hospitals in a particular area, 141
how many takes you will shoot of each shot, 114
hungry actors, 39
Hurricane Iniki, 148-150
"hurry up and wait", 72, 151
illustration talent is not required, 85

immerse themselves in the story (actors), 99
important camera angles, 85
important notes, 86
improvising (ad-lib), 152
independent filmmakers, 102, 110, 194, 206, 213
independent films, 31, 44, 53, 66, 193, 208, 178, 186, 192
industry standard, 62, 211
information on how to get funding for a film, 25
information on the internet, 118
information that might benefit your film, 100
instinct and strong navigational skills, 56
insurance, 69
ironclad resolve, 73
"in the can" (film), 99, 131
Jurassic Park, 148-150
Kauai (Hawaii), 148-150
keep it really small (when filming), 70
Kinko's, 108
knowledge of filmmaking is required, 25, 95
Kodak, 94, 113-116
labeling film cans, 75
lab fees (film), 83, 94, 177
Laptop (or Notebook) computer, 54, 117-118
Lara Croft: Tomb Raider, 183
lavalier microphones, 167-170
Laws of Gravity, 23
lay your feelings on the page, 30
lighting, 74
Lions Gate Studios, 62
Living End, The, 23
Location Scouting, 48-58
lodging in a small town, 128
logging the correct time code, 170-171

Los Angeles, California, 39
low budget film (movie), 29, 40, 43, 48, 68, 73, 94, 108, 121, 125, 131, 139, 151, 165, 182
MAKING PRINTS OF YOUR MOVIE, 211
MAKING TRAVEL ARRANGEMENTS, 116-129
managerial heavy lifting, 77
MIPCOM, 219
Mitchell Caverns, 55
Mojave Desert, 55-56
Matrix Revolutions, The, 183
Microsoft Word, 216
motel/hotel reservations, 121, 123-129
Mount Ranier, Washington, 50
movie, 22, 26, 28-29, 42, 45, 88, 99, 121, 174
Moviola, 196-198
"Mule Days" event (Bishop, California), 127
multi-tasking, 26, 138-139
Nagra tape recorders, 163-164
NATPE, 219
"natural" look, 172
natural sound, 169
never have *down time*, 72, 132
no-one has a monopoly on creativity, 28
omni directional (microphone), 169
optical track (sound), 211
Owens Valley (Eastern Sierras), 127, 160
PDF format, 15
Pickford, Mary, 181
portray *your* vision accurately, 69
Post-Production, 180-213
Pre-Production, 82-129
press package, 215-216
primary duties as Director, 144-147

Production, 130-179
professional filmmaker, 94, 221
PROPS AND COSTUMES, 84, 93, 108-112, 171-174
protect your film and DAT bag, 175-176
protect your film equipment at all times, 132
Pro Tools, 206
quality is your primary concern with film labs, 177-179
quick and easy to consume (meals), 125
REHEARSING WITH YOUR ACTORS, 103-104, 138, 155
RELEASE FORMS/CONTRACTS, 104-108
responsibilities to juggle, 129
Rudloff, Tex, 62
"run and gun" outfit, 70, 151, 163
SAFETY, 139-144
Sam's Club, 125
Santa Barbara Film Festival, The, 217-218
SCRIPT BREAKDOWN, 92-94
serious actors, 44-45
shooting formula, 151-154
shooting in a crowded public place, 169
Sin City, 23
Six Flags, 150
"smart" slate, 162
SOUND DESIGN AND MIXING, 205-211
Spielberg, Steven, 148-150
Spy Kids, 23
stay true to your vision, 54-56
Steadycam, 101, 156-158
Stick to the Script, 135-136
STORYBOARDING, 85-92
Sundance Film Festival, The, 21, 214, 216-219
take notes, 190

telecine machine, 203-204
"The Game" (film industry), 26
time code, 170-171
Tips for Getting Good Performances from Actors, 154-155
Tips for Writing a Low Budget Script, 30-34
TITLES AND CREDITS, 192-194
Toronto Film Festival, The, 214, 217-218
TRANSFERRING YOUR FILM TO VIDEO/DVD, 212-214
"two-pop" CD or DAT (final mix), 211
unspeakable grief, 191
"upright" or "flatbed" models (*Moviolas*), 196
videotape or DVD Master, 212
walkie-talkies, 75
Weather Channel, The, 119
Welles, Orson, 88
window copy transfer, 203-205
wireless microphones, 75, 167-168
work print, 197-201
YOU RETAIN ALL RIGHTS TO THE FILM, 107
your standards, 137
your story, 135
"zeppelin" (windscreen), 168
Ziploc bags, 175

Acknowledgements and References

. . . .

    I would like to thank Tex Rudloff, the head of Lions Gates Studios (in 1987) for the invaluable advice he gave me during an interview he granted me back in the late eighties. I was doing a *Senior project* term paper about how to make it in the film industry and he was kind enough to invite me to his office at Lions Gates Studios and talk to me about this subject. Meeting with him on that day opened my eyes to the fact that the film industry is a business that is made up of hard-working people just like any other industry, and that the *people* aspect of it will always be the most important part. Among many things, he told me that he would much rather hire a person that is easy to get along with than he would a person who is extremely talented, yet difficult to work with.

    Tex was working in the film industry when movies were still being invented as we know them today, and he has seen the Hollywood film industry transform from a fledgling industry to a multi-billion dollar industry. When I asked him to tell me the most important factor in becoming successful in the film industry, he told me this; getting along with other people is the key to success in the film industry. He then told me that there have been a whole lot of talented people in this world that were never successful for one reason or another, but he believed that more importantly most of the ones that are successful have one thing in common; they managed to administer a balance of creative and social skills throughout their careers. He said that it is very important for a person to be able to navigate the rough waters of the film industry with an even keel and a calm demeanor, or you will find that you are always in rough waters. It's hard to get things done when you are constantly fighting the rapids. A lot of people get chewed up and spit out.

While there are exceptions to the rule, for the most part difficult people find it very hard to succeed in life, even if they are very talented. There are different levels of success and different versions of it as well, but there is one thing that is certain; finding success is always easier when you search for it with a diplomatic approach. I have always remembered the advice of Tex Rudloff. It has helped me in numerous ways to get my films made with a very, very, low budget.

I would also like to thank all of the people that have supported me and my film career cause, as well as all the people who worked on all of my films over the years. From my early beginnings filming with an 8mm camera in my parent's back yard with my ten year old neighborhood friends, to the present day working with professional film crews, I have had the pleasure of working with some very talented and enjoyable people along the way. There are too many to mention, but they all know who they are. Thank you for the support and hard work you put in on my film projects, and thank you for the fun times.

ACKNOWLEDGEMENTS AND REFERENCES

As for the references; I wrote this book by drawing entirely on my own experiences as a filmmaker. At no time did I ever open another book or even go on the internet for sources. Any facts or events that are described in this book came from my own memory bank. The words just seemed to flow out like water over a swollen river gorge. There was no need to draw on any other sources as references for I have had enough experiences to fill several books on the subject of low budget filmmaking.

Any mention of famous people or famous films, or famous events can be credited to my film school education at California State University, Northridge, and to the education I received over the years on the film festival circuit.

Printed in the United States
100812LV00008B/149/A